A Playful Spirit

A Playful Spirit

Exploring the Theology, Philosophy, and Psychology of Play

Mark W. Teismann
with Lynn Weber

LEXINGTON BOOKS
Lanham • Boulder • New York • London

Published by Lexington Books
An imprint of The Rowman & Littlefield Publishing Group, Inc.
4501 Forbes Boulevard, Suite 200, Lanham, Maryland 20706
www.rowman.com

6 Tinworth Street, London SE11 5AL, United Kingdom

Copyright © 2020 The Rowman & Littlefield Publishing Group, Inc.

All rights reserved. No part of this book may be reproduced in any form or by any electronic or mechanical means, including information storage and retrieval systems, without written permission from the publisher, except by a reviewer who may quote passages in a review.

British Library Cataloguing in Publication Information Available

Library of Congress Cataloging-in-Publication Data Available

ISBN 9781793618412 (cloth)
ISBN 9781793618436 (pbk)
ISBN 9781793618429 (electronic)

Contents

Preface   vii
Lynn Weber

Acknowledgments   xi

Introduction   1

1   Everyday Play   9

2   Possibility Play   31

3   Dark Play   43

4   Flanking Play   57

5   Bright Play   75

6   Meditation: The Ultimate Play   101

7   Conclusion   115

8   Epilogue: The Final Hole   125

Appendix: How to Meditate   131

Select Bibliography   145

Index   151

About the Authors   157

Preface

Lynn Weber

The twentieth and twenty-first centuries battered the great narratives of religion and philosophy by drawing back the curtain on their contradictions and impermanence. In response, some people retreated into a regressive fundamentalism while others abandoned themselves to nihilism and cynicism. But Mark Teismann—an esteemed psychologist, therapist, theologian, and athlete—felt that there was another way, one that would honor our spiritual thirst as well as our shifting understanding of the world: the idea of spirituality as play. How it is possible to embrace spirituality in postmodern times was Mark's principal concern.

Mark spent many years thinking and writing about this idea, but his journey down the highways and byways of spiritual play was cut short by cancer. After Mark's passing, his best friend, Howard Waitzkin, and beloved wife, Ruth Jackson, passed on his notes and essays to me to edit and develop, resulting in this present volume.

This is, without a doubt, not quite the book that Mark would have produced. I found Mark to be an incredibly inventive and engaging writer, and my talents are more in organization and exposition. Mark was a great storyteller as well and passionate about his spiritual and philosophical wanderings. His scholarly knowledge was enormous—much vaster than is evident here. Still, I hope that this volume captures enough of Mark's genius and spirit to satisfy readers looking to understand and even to practice play as spirituality.

Mark's introduction outlines the traits of play—participation, fun, imagination, and liminality. In the chapters that follow, he takes the reader on a whirlwind ride through the different aspects of play and how they relate to spirituality: everyday play, possibility play, dark play, flanking play, and bright play. Mark draws on theologians and philosophers, memories and studies of childhood, developmental science, poets, and his long career as a psychotherapist to create in each chapter a deep understanding of how play informs our moral pursuits and spiritual yearnings.

In chapter 1, "Everyday Play," he traces how philosophers and theologians have conceived of play from ancient times to the present. In the nineteenth and twentieth centuries, child development specialists and thinkers like Jean Piaget, Sigmund Freud, Erik Erikson, and Donald Winnicott added a perspective based on psychology and biology. In recent years, studies of mass murderers and serial killers have added surprising insights into the role of play in moral development and healthy psychology.

Chapter 2, "Possibility Play," highlights the creative aspect of play and spirituality, one intimately linked to notions of freedom among figures as diverse as Heraclitus, Mihai Spariosu, Friedrich Schiller, and Edward Arlington Robinson. In particular, approaching our beliefs about God with a spirit of "as if" allows us to honor our spiritual traditions and insights while avoiding a rigid fundamentalism.

Mark explores the dark side of creativity and freedom when they are unconstrained by spirituality in chapter 3, "Dark Play." In its most benign form, it can be a type of frivolous, egocentric play like that of the famed Merry Pranksters. At its worst, play devolves into games, where exploring and imagining are overtaken by a fiercely competitive drive to dominate and conquer. This dark drive accounts for many of our worst impulses and societal ills: domination, manipulation, addiction, patriarchy, war, and cruelty. It can infect all human pursuits, from business to religion, with its incessant drive for power.

Chapter 4, "Flanking Play," describes a curious antidote to the dangers of dark play. It takes a deep dive into the philosophy of John Dewey and William James in addressing the dangers of addiction and obsession. Rather than trying to dominate the problem through the sheer force of will, these philosophers (along with the founder of Alcoholics Anonymous) recommend setting down one's weapons, disengaging with the concepts of fighting and winning, in favor of a playful approach of distraction and observation. Mark here introduces the practice of meditation as a flanking maneuver to abandon the metaphors of war and aggression and redirect us to a healthy and playful spirituality.

In chapter 5, "Bright Play," Mark analyzes our most direct practices of spirituality—the world's great religions, spiritual practices, and even theories of evolution and chaos. He addresses the playful sides of St. Francis, Meister Eckhart, the Besht, Martin Buber, the Buddha, the goddess Kali, and many others. Through their many spiritual practices, play becomes a beautiful vehicle of ego-transformation, the very heart of all spirituality.

Chapter 6, "Ultimate Play," takes a focused look at Buddhist meditation, which the author practiced. Meditation, Mark shows, offers a crystalline example of why play becomes a useful metaphor for understanding and practicing spirituality. He expounds on the bodhisattva as an ideal of compassion and ethical behavior rooted in the practices of meditation and emptiness.

A conclusion and epilogue summarize the book's tenets by touching on Mark's encounter with cancer. Here he shows how the practices of meditation and play accompanied him on his spiritual journey in the context of an incurable disease. The book's appendix gives interested readers a detailed description of how to approach the practice of meditation.

Acknowledgments

Heartfelt thanks go to Dean Birkenkamp, senior editor at Routledge, for putting me in touch with Howard and Ruth. In my long publishing career, Dean has been one of the editors most interested in producing quality work, and I'm honored that he thought of me when he embarked on what turned out to be many hours of work to bring Mark's book to light.

Thanks as well to Rolf Janke, executive editor at Rowman & Littlefield, who referred the book to Michael Gibson, senior acquisitions editor at Lexington Books. Michael, assistant editor Mikayla Mislak, and publisher Julie Kirsch at Lexington Books have been a dream to work with, as kind and fun as they are talented and efficient. I'm so grateful for their skill and collegiality.

Howard Waitzkin was Mark's closest friend, colleague, and meditation partner. He is also a physician, sociologist, and activist. Before he died, Mark honored Howard by sharing the notes he had written for this book. Though Mark had not asked for any particular action on his notes, Howard was inspired by what he read and approached Mark's beloved wife, Ruth Jackson, about developing these writings into a book. Ruth, a naturopath, therapist, and feminist leader, concurred. Together, they made Mark's dream a reality. Their talent, compassion, and dedication made this volume possible and gave the world an invaluable window into the mind and heart of the friend and husband that they loved so dearly.

Introduction

When I was a child attending Catholic elementary school, my favorite teacher was Sister Fabian. While many of the nuns were rigid and dogmatic, Sister Fabian had a lively spirit and open heart. Perhaps that's why one day when I was goofing off with friends in the back of the room, she singled me out with the probing query, "Tell me, Mark—what do you think the Holy Spirit is like?" And why I felt free enough to blurt out, "The Holy Spirit plays!"

I'm not sure what made me say that, but my life since then has borne out an intense interest in both spirituality and play. As the years have gone by, the religion of my youth has many times let me down. But neither spirituality nor play has lost its fruitfulness.

In this book, I seek to explore how play might serve as a potent metaphor for our spiritual lives and a vehicle of spiritual growth. This introduction begins with a discussion of the spiritual challenges of our age. Then it moves toward a discussion of play and why it might be a fitting metaphor for the spiritual journey, not in an ethereal way but one that offers everyday meaning, a basis for care of others, and most of all a sense of hope and joy. Finally, it concludes with an introduction to what I call the "Five Windows of Spirit as Play," which will serve as a framework for the rest of the book.

Along the way we'll look at related issues: How do we account for, integrate, and deeply respect humanity's vast diversity of religions and their subdivisions, as well as their particular views of reality, their rituals, dogmas, emphases, and practices? What cultural events and strains of thinking dispose us to question, feel defensive about, and seek alternatives relative to the religious traditions of our childhood? Is there a thread that might weave from our past beliefs through our present searching and into a meaningful future? It turns out that the concept of play may very well offer a way to sort through these dilemmas.

THE CRISIS OF CONTEMPORARY SPIRITUALITY

We live in an information-saturated, contradictory, question-filled postmodern world. Along with the information revolution has come an unprecedented exposure to other ways of life. We know cultures other than our own in ways that would have been impossible a hundred years ago. Documentaries take us intimately into the lives of people who seem nothing like us. Globalization brings people from other countries to our workplaces and us to theirs.

These perspectives have enriched our lives greatly. But like all knowledge, it complicates things. Many of us grew up in relatively homogenous cultures (for me, white, suburban, middle class, Catholic, and Midwestern), and the certainty of such an upbringing can be shaken by such wide exposure to the world. With so many approaches to God, how can we know ours is right? Or for that matter, that any one is right? The plurality of religion suggests a truth problem.

But globalization and the Information Revolution constitute just one challenge for traditional religion. The twentieth century saw unprecedented and often deeply disturbing changes in society, politics, and culture. Two of the most destructive wars in human history happened within fifty years of each other in the first half of the twentieth century—and both initiated by a country, Germany, that had been considered the height of civilization—the land of Goethe and Beethoven. Soon after, idealistic Americans who fought for workers' rights were faced with the depravities of the Stalin-era Soviet Union, for which they'd held high hopes. And the Cold War had children quivering under their desks for nuclear disaster drills.

The unleashing of nuclear power helped people recognize technology for the double-edged sword it was, offering the promise of scientific progress (nuclear power, the space program, and medical breakthroughs) but also the insanity of mass destruction. In fact, the entire struggle of the Cold War left many Americans troubled by the apparent lack of universality of ideals they had been weaned on. The nonaligned movement showed that even independent countries were suspicious of American power and the depredations of colonialism. And then there was Joseph McCarthy and the terrible cloud of suspicion he created over fellow citizens. My father hated McCarthy and the HUAC, which left me lying in bed wondering if my father was a communist.

As the century wore on, globalization began to take its toll economically as well, as blue-collar industries like steel and auto moved production abroad and American workers scrambled to maintain a middle-class lifestyle. Crises in banking revealed a frailty in our economic system previously undetected. In recent years, the specter of banking collapse has eroded Americans' sense of individual power and agency, and as the traditional labor market collapsed, the new gig economy has people working harder but feeling less secure.

What all of these things have in common is a heightened sense of uncertainty. The union jobs our fathers had would not be there for us. The stability of a civilized society could be turned inside out by fascism. Science drilled potholes in our concept of faith.[1] And the truisms and solid faith of our childhood now looked suspiciously like cultural preferences. As the twenty-first century dawned, widespread child sexual abuse by Catholic priests was uncovered, striking a blow to one of the most solid and time-tested institutions in the world. And the great American union—whose progress and stability seemed indestructible—began to fracture amid intense culture wars over abortion and other issues.

The reaction to this great uncertainty has been varied. Some continue to seek certainty and comfort in traditional religion. Fundamentalists may shut the doors of their spiritual bomb shelters, made of premodern debris torn to shreds by the bombardment of twentieth-century history. They huddle together with others in their insulated worlds, denying the reality outside their doors. Others return to the religions of their childhood and find renewed hope in a more loving and open version of their faith.

If the fear or uncertainty is great enough and clear and rational explanation and direction are unavailable or unappreciated, some turn to a savior—a trickster or messiah character—who appears to hold the promise of certainty or security. Or the fearful will turn to the supernatural when the natural, rational explanation and direction are unavailable or unappreciated whether because of immaturity or ignorance.

Others abandon traditional religion altogether, finding it lacking for a number of reasons: scandals by clergy, historical wrongs, hypocrisy, or simply its inability to address the big questions of life, especially the problem of evil and unnecessary suffering. Those who turn from their culture's traditional faith may dabble in world religions without committing themselves, or simply turn away from spirituality completely. Some honestly say they don't know if there is a God, whether religion is for the better or worse, and just try to do what seems right. Still others, without changing their dogmatic disposition, assert an intolerant atheism.

THE POSTMODERN REACTION

The spirit of the age described above can perhaps most accurately be described as postmodern. Postmodernism recognizes how certainties rise and fall and how no one statement, belief, or perspective can ever wholly contain the truth. Like a game of King of the Mountain, one perspective reigns supreme until toppled by another. This serious game of one-upmanship goes on and on with one after another idea ascending to the top of the mountain, often with the help of social, political, and economic factors or even manipulations. The same is true of political, social, psychological, and economic thought. Each school and its champions climb to the mountain and enjoy their brief supremacy only to be toppled eventually.

Postmodern thought posits that there is no center, no constant presence, no absolute or final concept on which to stand with any assurance. There is only the continual expression of the free play of ideas and their linguistic signs, which, of course, are just another perspective of reality. Skepticism, and even nihilism, may accompany this realization.

The lack of a fixed center means that moral reasoning in modernity has become incoherent.[2] In the past, we could turn to tradition for our rules of engagement, but the Enlightenment began a slow turning from outside traditions and authorities in favor of individual reasoning. From Descartes' *cogito ergo sum* to Tevye's Fiddler on the Roof, we have questioned the traditions that handed us the rulebook and took out pen and paper to draft new rules grounded in rationality. But when we recognize that rational modernity is also a tradition, like the Enlightenment, we enter postmodern thought. Postmodern thought stands against the repression of unquestioned authority and for the freedom of humankind, but recognizes that it is itself an authority in disguise, one with its own biases and limitations.

The rabbit hole of postmodernism can trigger many responses. One response, mentioned above, is simply to retreat from it, to reject the insights that it offers, and to take refuge in the doctrinal and moral absolutes of tradition. In the context of our postmodern world, this requires a rigid opposition to anything that might acknowledge doubt or perspective or multiplicity.

Another response is to give into skepticism and cynicism, to insist that nothing can be known and nothing can be concluded, certainly not in the moral realm. Those who embrace this approach will always win the argument because they take no stand, only undermine other approaches. Their tactic is to play good defense, not a good offense. Unfortunately their game always ends in a 0–0 tie with nothing, zero, being accomplished. Skepticism is an invaluable tool in some ways. It is a good tool against fanaticism and irrationality. It challenges the center and opens to the margins. It encourages the play of other voices, looks beyond the paradigmatic, and embraces what all people can celebrate. It undermines efforts to silence justice and freedom seeking. But it is a useful tool, not a blueprint for moral life. It offers corrective value, but not creative import. It emphasizes subversive safety, not risk; the same, not better; the usual, not possibility; and the status quo, not change.

Yet another response is to embrace the fragmentation of our previously coherent moral traditions. Our lives become smorgasbords of endless offerings that are left to individual taste, often void of nourishing critique and reflection. We are a culture that dabbles, trying this and that, always discovering one more taste to delight the spiritual palate. We may look for gurus, ministers who we feel personally touch our souls as opposed to simply offering rules or traditions. When one new guru or movement stops piquing our appetite, we simply move on to the next.

But perhaps there is a way to embrace the realities of postmodernism—the untrustworthiness of our grand narratives, the importance of understanding the perspectives of others, and the knowledge of our fallibility—without becoming lost in them. I believe there is such a way, and it is this that I call "play." Play's relevance to our contemporary challenges is multifaceted and will take up the bulk of this volume. But let's start by considering what play is, exactly. Let's play with *play*.

DEFINING PLAY

"Play" is a simple word that grows more complex the more you think about it. It covers everything from a children's game of tag to a grandmaster chess tournament, from playing classical piano to playing pat-a-cake with an infant, and from a novelist playing with words to lovers playacting in bed. But in all these scenarios, there are some constants that make play what it is.

First, play is participation. It is something you do, not something you receive or observe. And we humans like to do things—we were made with creative impulses and are happiest when we are doing the things that come naturally to us.

This leads us to our second definition: Play is fun. Play combines effort with reward, rewards that are fairly close to immediate. Some rewards can be the product of play, but—to be play—the activity must also be its own reward. We *want* to play. If we don't want to do it, it probably isn't play.

Third, play is imaginative. We are not reciting a doctrine or performing a ritual. We are not enacting a series of steps that can only have one outcome. There may be rules, but those rules are not deterministic, not instructions so much as parameters. Within true play, there will always be the new, the unexpected, and the indeterminate.

Combining these three characteristics leads us to another perspective: play is "in-between." The fancy philosophical term would be "liminal," participating in or existing between two realities. The word "liminality" is based on the Latin *limens*, which means "threshold." It was first proposed by anthropologist Arnold van Gennep to describe tribal rites of passages, those periods of testing that divide childhood from adulthood in small-scale societies. This narrow definition was expanded by Victor Turner in his 1967 essay "Betwixt and Between: The Liminal Period in Rites of Passage."[3] Richard Rohr explained it this way: "It is when you have left the tried and true, but have not yet been able to replace it with anything else. It is when you are between your old comfort zone and any possible new answer."[4]

Now liminality is used to describe all sorts of experiences, periods, and spaces that have the quality of being set apart—set apart from the everyday or positioned between opposites or extremes. It's the engagement between dating and marriage. It's the sacred space of the church or temple situated between heaven and earth. It's the figure of the trickster, neither hero nor villain. And it can be play, the experience of effortful fun that lies between work and repose.

The liminality and ambiguity of play exist in so many ways. There is the "between" of the desire for the goal and the realization of the goal. Between challenge and outcome, thinking and conclusion, Apollonian and Dionysian, individual action and group action, rules and flexibility, and danger and safety. How many times have we heard from parents, during a particularly unruly bout of play, "Somebody's gonna get hurt!" And how many times has seemingly good-natured roughhousing between kids turned, somewhere in the middle, into outright aggression? Think, too, of the line between college students partying and alcoholism: When does relatively harmless fun turn into reckless behavior or addiction?

In this aspect, liminality calls to mind the philosophical concept of *aporia*. Harking back to Plato, aporia generally refers to a state of mental immobilization, of "being at a loss." It's what happened to Socrates' students when he pressed them with ever more penetrating questions and they finally had no answers. We have our initial idea on the one hand and a cogent critique on the other; for at least a moment we live in that in-between space where we cannot reconcile the two and yet can't give either one up.

Aporia usually refers to being intellectually stymied, but our lives are filled with moments of "existential aporia." When it's been five years, but still your boyfriend hasn't proposed. When you've graduated from college and have no idea what kind of job you should look for. When your seemingly solid marriage suddenly goes off the rails. Or you've been laid off and don't know who you are without your career success.

Learning to live "in-between"—in this state of uncertainty—may be the single most important skill for fostering and maintaining mental health. When an occupational counselor recommends that the client make "'looking for a job' your job," she is grounding the client in the in-between as a reality. She recommends routines, schedules that will provide structure and discipline and focus to the person. Same with psychotherapy. When therapists like me have clients who are unmoored by events, we try to ground them in a role with specific behaviors, like how to meet and evaluate a new partner.

Those who can tolerate the ambiguity do well in the end. Others become overwhelmed with the uncertainty and seek resolution or escape in any way possible. Richard Rohr points out the risks of the liminal state: "If you are not trained in how to hold anxiety, how to live with ambiguity, how to entrust and wait, you will run [to] anything to flee this terrible cloud of unknowing."[5] This fleeing may be into negative escape mechanisms like fundamentalism or nihilism or addiction or repression. Ambiguity and liminality can be very difficult. Think of the agony of parents whose children have gone missing. Years may pass and they still they say, "I just want to know if he's dead or alive. Even if he's dead, I just want to know."

This is the cruel side of liminality, but the life-giving side of liminality is about potential and experience and acceptance. It is about mourning the loss of a job opportunity in another city, and then rejoicing six months later when you find your true love in the city you're in. It's about not getting into your top college, and then being discovered by a writing instructor at your second choice. But more than having one door close and another open, it's a deep acceptance of the uncertainty that is so much a part of life itself. And play can be a celebration of this, a celebration of impermanence, in fact, of change itself. It can be a way of accepting the postmodern uncertainty about God and morality without giving into nihilism or pure skepticism. Aristotle and Aquinas recognized play as existing somewhere between seriousness and foolishness. Aquinas developed Aristotle's *eutrapelia*, which loosely translated means "hanging loose," as the synthesis between "boringly serious" and "ridiculously silly." It is echoed in Diogenes Laertius's description of Heraclitus as "grave-merry" man and Xenophon's idealization of Socrates as "merry-serious." In the context of these ancients, play is the "in-between world" that brings a virtuous balance to living within reality. It is a hyphen between the serious and trivial that gives meaning to life.[6] And it may be just the key to the spiritual challenges of our times.

PLAY AS POSTMODERN SPIRITUALITY: THE FIVE WINDOWS

In the years since I blurted out "The Holy Spirit plays!" in elementary school, I have been struck over and over again how the characteristics of play fit our spiritual needs in a time of postmodern fragmentation and uncertainty. As an activity that encompasses creativity, power, love, and joy, it has an almost unparalleled capacity to address and accommodate all of the pieces of spiritual life. In the chapters that follow, we will look at play through what I call the Five Windows. The Five Windows of spiritual play are as follows:

1. Everyday Play
2. Possibility Play

3. Dark Play
4. Flanking Play
5. Bright Play

Through these Five Windows, we can see how play offers a response to the postmodern crisis that requires neither rigidity nor skepticism nor dabbling. How play, in fact, offers an approach to God.

NOTES

1. Neuroscience has begun to map the areas of the mind associated with faith—and how they can be manipulated. See the appendix for a fuller discussion of this development.

2. Alasdair C. MacIntyre and Kelvin Knight, *The MacIntyre Reader,* ed. Kelvin Knight (Cambridge: Polity Press, 1998).

3. Victor Turner, *The Forest of Symbols* (Ithaca, NY: Cornell University Press, 1967).

4. Quoted in Carrie Barron, "Creativity and the Liminal Space," *Psychology Today*, June 4, 2013.

5. Quoted in Barron, "Creativity and the Liminal Space."

6. Robert Miller, "Zen and the Media," *Tirra Lirra: The Australian Independent Contemporary Magazine* 6, nos. 2–3 (1996): 8–12.

Chapter 1

Everyday Play

I joined the workforce when I was ten. Before then, work and play were the same. Maybe it was my German genes, because making my bed and keeping my room clean felt good. Beating previous time records when I vacuumed the living room and cleaned the bathroom was a game and helping my mom with my baby sister, a pure delight. I enjoyed learning, so school wasn't work either. Adults thought work and play were different, but it didn't feel that way to me. Work, like play, was something you just did—and had fun doing.

One summer day in 1953, this all changed. While pulling the lawn mower out of my grandparent's garage, I broke a window pane. Grandpa was coming home for dinner and I wanted to make it up to him. To my ten-year-old mind, the way to do this was to mow the outline of the face of Mickey Mouse, my favorite cartoon character, onto the front lawn.

As I stood atop a stepladder and admired my creation, Grandpa drove his black 1947 Ford into the yard. As he climbed out, I exclaimed, "Look Grandpa, I made Mickey Mouse for you. Oh, and I'm sorry I broke the window," pointing toward the garage.

My 6'6" grandfather did not look happy with my offering. "What's this?" pointing to the mouse. "Do you think life's a game? Do your work now, play later! And clean up that broken glass! Now!"

After I cleaned up the shards in the garage, my grandfather reemerged from the house, his anger expended, no doubt in part because of my grandmother's dinner offerings. He walked toward me with a gentle expression and said, "Let me show you how to cut grass." And as I mowed over Mickey with neat, straight lines, I dutifully marched into the adult world, leaving something of my childhood behind.

My grandfather was a hard-working, no-nonsense man. A skilled laborer, he believed that work put food on the table, clothes on our backs, and a roof over our heads. It developed character, paid bills, and created wealth, which in turn provided financial security and the hope of being free from work one day. He believed that good work elevated the human spirit because it transcended mere personal gain by contributing to one's family and the common good. He believed, as Freud did, that worthy work gives meaning to one's life.

I appreciated and respected my grandfather. But the separation of work and play always felt uncomfortable to me. I just didn't see why practicality and efficiency needed to be divorced from fun and imagination. Even as I moved the lawnmower over my Mickey design, I secretly imagined that I was a low-flying airplane with sharp propellers and razor wings cutting off the treetops of a great grass forest and feeding the aboriginal bugs below.

PLAY IN EVERYDAY LIFE

Everyone wants work to be play and serious effort to be fun. Experience tells us that the smaller the split between work and play, the greater the happiness. Undoubtedly, our lives would be more joyful and meaningful if we had this play-work unity. But most of us have only a play-work *overlap*, not a play-work unity. Cell phones jerk us from lunch with friends and tennis with buddies. We prepare income tax while watching the NBA playoffs and lug our laptops on vacations and weekend getaways. We feel strangely guilty when we play or indulge in a moment of leisure. Our leisure hours are spent on useful projects like home repair and maintenance. Although we plan, save, and look forward to vacations, we bring along work in our hands, or at least in our heads. Not seriously doing something serious makes us uncomfortable. Like my grandfather, we are uneasy with play.

In addition, we believe deep down that our work, not our play, determines our psychosocial value. We identify ourselves with what we do for a living and are rewarded accordingly with social and financial status. When is the last time a conversation at a party began with, "What's your play?" rather than "What's your job?" We are suspicious of play as well because it sometimes tips over into excess—philandering or alcoholism or drug addiction. Unruly play is addictive in all shades of obsession and compulsion. It is the ceaseless recreation of shopaholics, computer game addicts, sport nuts, porn seekers, and Facebook narcissists. In this dark way, play erodes character and squanders potential—and makes us deeply wary.

In the relentless pursuit of achievement, work becomes the measure of our success and the focus of our mental and emotional life. In a 2014 Gallup poll, 40 percent of U.S. employees said they work more than fifty hours each week, while 20 percent put in more than sixty hours.[1] And Americans receive—and use—significantly less vacation than workers in other countries.[2] These weary statistics so permeate our lives that workers talk of needing "downtime," as if they were machines.[3]

If play-work harmony has become a luxury that only a few lucky individuals can have and play-work overlap the fate of the rest of us, we have a long history that helps explain why. Philosophy, theology, and even our innate impulses often collude to separate and prioritize work. But along the way, some thinkers have helped us see play differently.

ANCIENT PERSPECTIVES: SLICING, STACKING, AND SUBORDINATING PLAY

Our world seems made up of differences. We walk through our backyard and see grass, bugs, birds, and our child playing with the family cat. They all seem different from us and from one another. Whether these differences are subjectively invented or objectively noted, whether these distinctions are illusions or facts, daily living disposes us to separate reality into parts.

Our world also seems organized up and down. During our backyard walk we see bugs munching on grass, birds munching on bugs, and—to our chagrin—the cat munching on a chickadee. We see hierarchies everywhere: in nature's food chain, intelligence, societies, and, if religious, in the Creator's plan. Whether we create it or whether it is created for us, hierarchy seems indisputable.

Our view of reality as separate, with levels, dovetails with our knack to think critically. Critical thinking builds on our sense that reality is divided and ranked and makes judgments about those divisions and rankings. Critical thinking not only slices and stacks reality, it also scrutinizes and stipulates what-goes-where on the hierarchal ladder. Separating and ordering play and work, then, seems just another case of what we do every day. We separate and make judgments about what is more or less important to daily living. But this does not explain why work seems to rank above play, until we examine critical thinking a little more.

In our culture we routinely identify critical thinking with work but not with play. Unlike work, play does not require critical thought, in fact, thinking seems contrary to play. We equate play with a spontaneous, whole body, intuitive, and free process, unlike critical thinking's measured, cerebral deductions. Similar to work, critical thinking is a serious, practical, necessary, and "real world" activity, which revolves in a very different orbit than the fun, frivolity, fantasy, and freedom of the play world.

Since critical thinking sides with serious work and seems to conflict with play, we can easily see why critical thinking judges work superior to play. This judgment is reinforced by economic reality.

Unproductive Play

Unlike work, play has no direct value to productivity. It may offer relief and refreshment so we can work better, but its benefits are only indirect. Further, except for the likes of gifted artists and athletes, play offers no monetary gain to the player. Play doesn't make money, rather it drains money. We spend our money on our children so they can play. We save and splurge on vacations and equipment so we can play. Play doesn't replenish our financial resources—it depletes them.

Our negative attitudes toward the financially advantaged who live to play further suggest why we regard productive work as superior to play. We bristle when we read that a baseball player is making $250 million. We feel contempt toward "trust fund babies" supported by their parents' financial windfalls. We despise thieves who think work is for suckers. We disdain the entitlements of welfare recipients and scoff at the indulgences of playboys and playgirls. Honest, serious work—not play—buys goods and services. Workers—not players—build healthy economies, societies, and moral character.

Immoral Play

The early Fathers of Christianity not only severed and subordinated play, they believed it was useless and even detrimental to spiritual life. Under the heavy blade of ascetic seriousness, the great saints Paul, Augustine, Ambrose, and Chrysostom mowed down Jesus's encouragement that we become as children in order to attain the Kingdom. My grandfather could have quoted Paul (1 Corinthians 13:11) in his initiation rite: "When I was a child, I spoke like a child, I thought like a child, I reasoned like a child. When I became a man, I gave up childish ways."

Augustine, confessing his earlier indulgences, argued that a life of play was vanity. In his commentary on Psalm 38, he wrote, "As they are, our lives are perilous comedies of play. For it is written: Nothing but vanity is such a life." Ambrose also believed that a playful life should be squelched. Supporting his contention, he quoted Luke 6:25: "Woe to you who laugh, for you shall mourn and weep." But the harshest was Chrysostom, who used Luke's quote to equate play with the devil's work: "This world is not a theater in which we can laugh. We are not assembled together in order to burst into peals of laughter. Rather we are here to weep for our sins! Some of you will say: 'I prefer that God gives me a chance to laugh and joke.' Is there anything more childish than thinking this way? It is not God who gives us the chance to play, it is the devil!"[4]

Perhaps these saints were only objecting to play that promotes immoral and irresponsible behavior. But the Christian pietist Johann Tollner left little doubt of his wish to raze *all* play. He wrote, "Play of whatever sort should be forbidden in all evangelical schools, and its vanity and folly should be explained to children with warnings of how play turns the mind away from God and eternal life, and works destruction on their immortal souls."[5]

Early Christians believed the end of the world was imminent. Later Christians, seeing doomsday delayed, emphasized life's transience. The urgent or perpetual work of preparing for heaven brooked no frivolity. Death loomed and the serious business of saving one's soul meant repressing play.

These Christians connected play to bodily pleasure, which was the antithesis of care for the soul. Hard, honest, money-making work invited godliness and grounded the Protestant ethic. Work, not play, assisted the journey to eternal life. If heaven was to be the immortal soul's destiny, the devil had to be countered, and the mortal body and its play subverted.

Balancing Play

Glancing at Aristotle, we can see where these party poopers may have gotten their ideas for torching play. For instance, in *Ethics* (X.6), Aristotle left little doubt about play's junior place: "Serious things are intrinsically better than funny or amusing things" and "to make serious business of amusement and to dissipate days of labor are the height of folly and childishness." Many early Christians regarded Aristotle as their philosophical champion. Isolating these words, they stoked the fires of their anti-play campaigns.

However, a further reading tells a different story. Aristotle subordinated play but also saw its utility for a balanced life. In the same passage, he stated, "Play so that you may be serious." St. Thomas Aquinas, who built his philosophy on Aristotle's rationality, saw play as a counterbalance to becoming too serious. He wrote in the *Summa Theologiae,* "Now such like words or deeds wherein nothing further is sought than the soul's delight, are called playful or humorous. Hence it is necessary at times to make use of them, in order to give rest, as it were, to the soul." Aquinas and Aristotle, like Plato who was Aristotle's mentor, viewed play as giving balance to rationality and serious work.

Plato, who employed play in his philosophy, affirmed this balancing function. In his *Sixth Epistle* (323D) he urged his followers to "to live the life of philosophy in gentlemanly earnest, but with the playfulness that is the sister of solemnity." This seriousness-play balance was also seen in *Laws* III (695A) when he called the philosophical pursuit of justice an "old man's sober game of play." Plato encouraged this balance in both the *Republic* and *Laws*, when he argued that the primary purpose of play was the education of youth.[6]

Plato's mentor was Socrates, and in Socrates' teaching—the famous Socratic method of question and answer and challenge—we see the great philosopher engaging in his own type of play. Some of his followers "played along" and some threw a tantrum. They wanted resolution and closure, not critique and alternative thought. Some were more invested in their egos than the playfulness of the speculative journey. Bruised by Socrates' incessant challenges, Thrasymachus called him an ugly stingray! The sophist blowhard Euthyphro stormed out of class! If Thrasymachus and Euthyphro represent, in some way, the refusal to attend to subtleties and complexities, much like people today who retreat into an inflexible religious traditionalism, others, like the skeptic Meno, are more like the postmodernists and nihilists, taking uncertainty to the extreme, questioning whether we can and know anything at all.

Socrates's play was deeply ethical. He was a team player, indifferent to personal gain. For this truly great thinker, his field of play was the universe itself; his team was all humankind, whom he cared for deeply; and the goal of the good life for all was what motivated and inspired him. He wanted everyone to have fun playing this serious game of life. He is today alternately called the father of metaphysics and the father of skepticism, but as represented by Plato, he advocated both, siding with neither. He walked the middle line between certainty and uncertainty. He pursued the metaphysical good, true, and beautiful with honest skepticism. His Socratic method was not serving a burger and fries to fill up hungry seekers, but helping them work up a hunger that itself would nourish their souls. When he would give his followers a full meal, it was so that they could have a taste of the subtle and sublime involved in soulful dining.

Plato, Aristotle, and Aquinas were not opposed to play. They, like my grandfather, simply wanted play on the right step of reality's ladder. They looked at the sliced and stacked nature of reality and judged play as a lower yet valuable rung, one that helped humanity ascend to a balanced and noble seriousness. This seriousness then became the next step up toward the higher rungs of philosophy, justice, and reason, which became the scaffolding for constructing enlightened minds and sturdy republics. Play, like women and sexuality, was a lower, although a useful and necessary rung for building a better reality.

TWENTIETH-CENTURY PERSPECTIVES: PLAY AS FUNCTIONAL

The "rung view" of play—in which play rests far below other activities, either because it is unproductive, merely instrumental, or even evil—has been challenged as the centuries have passed. Our current views on play have been influenced by some of the great thinkers of the twentieth century. Although some of these thinkers still see play in a utilitarian light, even then it functions as an integral, organic part of our psyche and development rather than a distinct activity that should—or even can—be compartmentalized or shunned.

Edouard Claparede

In 1905 the Swiss psychologist Edouard Claparede wrote a book about children's play called *Experimental Pedagogy and the Psychology of the Child* (translated into English in 1911). In it he examined Plato, Aristotle, and Darwin and other works of philosophy, psychology, and anthropology. Claparede's guiding question was this: "Of what use is childhood?" Examining the usefulness of play, he proposed three theories of play: atavism, relaxation, and relief, as foils for his own theory, which was that play's basic function was preparing the child for mature adulthood.[7]

Atavism sees children's play like the tail of a tadpole. This theory, influenced by Darwin, notes play's presence in animals and suggests that children's play and its function seem to be throwbacks to early evolution. Play is a pre-rational drive that is pleasurable, impulsive, immature, and controlled by instinct. As the child grows and rationality takes over, the needless tail of play disappears. Consequently, play becomes useless and even regressive for the mature adult, a view our anti-play ancient and medieval Christians would endorse. This theory's remnants appear in Jungian psychology's *puer aeternas*, "the eternal boy," which denotes immature men who wiggle away from responsibility.

The relaxation theory evokes the old Coca-Cola slogan: "The pause that refreshes." This theory suggests that we play because we need a break. A change of pace helps us work more efficiently. This is Aristotle's "play so you may be serious" notion that views play as a balancing respite that enhances productive work and thought. Most Americans think about leisure this way. They think in terms of "breaks" and vacations designed to revitalize their work efforts.

This theory also reflects Americans' puritanical distrust of play when it's not serving seriousness and work. If we are not playing to work better, then we are "goofing off." Play must have some useful, serious reason; otherwise it leads to dissipation. Cindy Aron in her book *Working at Play* noted this distinction. Americans tended to slip into debauchery during their seaside vacations and journeys to fashionable spas. To counter this licentious amusement, reformers created recreational alternatives, in the forms of religious camps, chautauquas, self-improvement resorts, and educational world fairs. These and other health-related sabbaticals refocused vacation play on serious intellectual, religious, and therapeutic benefits.[8] Play was suspect if it did not lead to a useful good.

The third use for play that Claparede mentions—relief—understood play as venting. Here, play is like a release valve of an overheated pressure cooker. When a child plays, she expends excess energy, which calms her mind and body. Parents with hyperactive children might endorse this theory. Play regulates and reestablishes equilibrium by hissing off excess pressure. Exercise quells anxiety and counters depression by relieving tension. At day's end, we like to exercise and "chill out," easing the duress of serious work.

In the end, Claparede thought these theories useful but superficial. He believed that a more robust, functional theory was that play prepared children for adulthood. Reflecting Plato, Claparede viewed play as practice for the serious business of adulthood.

Play is the child's work for Claparede. It teaches the child, primarily through imitation, how to master social, psychological, and physical tasks. Through games, toys, and role-taking, the child practices by mimicking adult behavior, thereby mastering skills and strategies. In this relatively safe, nonserious, developmental period and through trial and error, the child learns how to become an adult. So strongly did Claparede assert play's function in a child's maturation that he believed insufficient or improper play arrested this development. In various combinations and emphases, his play theories can be found woven through all developmental theories, including those of Piaget, Freud, and Erikson.

Sigmund Freud

Freud's 1920 essay "Beyond the Pleasure Principle" set out his own theory of children's play.[9] Freud understood play as part of the psychic hydraulics of decreasing tension and increasing pleasure. He thought appropriate gratification or pleasure to be humanity's goal and play as one vehicle for getting there. For Freud, play prepared the child for adulthood through compensation.

When a child feels bored or anxious and fails to receive pleasure or comfort from a mother figure, he seeks compensatory or substitute pleasure from other sources through imaginative play. The child's ungratified bodily pleasure and accompanying frustration ignite the fires of imaginative play, which lead to alternative pleasures. Rather than remaining helplessly and anxiously passive, the child actively plays, turning the unpleasant circumstances into pleasurable games, often with satisfying outcomes. Freud might interpret my Mickey Mouse creation as such a compensation. Instead of dreading my grandfather's angry disappointment over the broken window, I compensated for my anxiety by mowing a Mickey Mouse. After my grandfather's reprimand, I put aside play long enough to clean up the glass.

Freud's play bubbles in a cauldron of anxiety. He views reality as a tense conflict, boiling with frustration and struggle and steaming with self-deception. For Freud, life is hard and saturated with opposing needs and drives that seek a refreshing pause through gratification. His functions of play reflect many of Claparede's theories, in that play releases tension, relaxes, and prepares the child for life's inevitable strife. Freud and Claparede do not credit one another, but their similarities are obvious. By mastering frustration and redirecting energy toward alternative pleasures, play prepares the child for managing the inevitable obstacles of life. Freud's play is palliative in that it relieves anxiety. It is also therapeutic, in that it evokes imagination as an important tool that encourages self-awareness, as well as problem-solving and communication skills, all of which help the tadpole swim into adult froghood. Play therapy, psychodrama, gestalt therapy, and other experiential therapies have all been directly or indirectly influenced by Freud's theory of play.

We find ideas of compensatory play as early as 1908, when Freud proposed a connection between a child's daydreaming and creative activity. A child daydreams like an artist creates. He theorized that both the child and the artist play out their stymied desires through imaginative expression. The child daydreams of being a prince or princess, while the artist daydreams an image and gives it creative form. Both child and artist draw on the energy of their frustrated wishes and, through play, master this discomfort and lionize it with eloquence. For Freud, the play that triggers a child's fantasy and make-believe games is the same play that finds an outlet as an Emily Dickinson poem or a van Gogh landscape.[10]

George Herbert Mead

George Herbert Mead, the eminent sociologist of the early twentieth century, also wrote about how play develops social consciousness, most notably in his 1934 volume *Mind, Self and Society*.[11] For Mead, as the child moves from playing play to playing games, she develops roles, rules, and a sense of self. In the initial stage, little Mary, for example, imitates her mother, an airline pilot, by taking on the same role. Initially Mary doesn't play any organized games, she only pretends to be a pilot. When she comes into contact with her friend Jane, who wants to be a physician, she realizes their role differences. This difference in roles alerts Mary and Jane that they are different "selves." Through contact, they each begin to integrate what it means to have a self by interacting through different roles.

Gradually Mary, as pilot, begins to play with Jane, as physician. In order to play together, both have to discipline their "selves" according to rules that respect one another's chosen role. Rules fascinate children and govern how they can both maintain their role/self and successfully play together. One day,

Mary will be a pilot flying Jane to a make-believe disaster area where she will put Band-Aids on victims. The next day, Jane will take care of Mary's cold with make-believe cough syrup so she can fly passengers to Hawaii. The rules are often made up on the fly and the games change quickly, often with more complexity. This rule-making and rule-mastering give each child a rudimentary empathy, self-esteem, and the confidence to go further.

In the next stage, which Mead calls "the generalized other," there is an awareness of all other rules and roles that organized the play of other children. Games become more organized, disciplined, and governed by increasingly complex rules. The rules of play help people remember that they are social, that is, that they have responsibilities to others, not just themselves. At this game stage, teams develop around communal games, such as baseball. This game stage becomes increasingly more socially complex and organized as it moves into later development. Eventually relationships move from teams to the serious interactions of everyday life, which Mead called "social games." With the mastery of these socially complex relationships, Mary and Jane graduate to adulthood where they play what Mead calls "the game of life itself."

Johan Huizinga

Johan Huizinga's *Homo Ludens* (1938) was another milestone volume for the growing twentieth-century meditation on play. Huizinga rejects the usefulness of play, noting that even animals play, without any moral or psychological significance to it. Huizinga believed that the justification for play came down to one irreducible concept: fun.

Because of the universality of play, Huizinga wrote that humankind should be understood as *homo ludens* (Man the Player) as much as *homo sapiens* (Man the Thinker) and *homo faber* (Man the Maker). For him, play is the essential element of almost any kind of cultural activity: not just sport but love, art, ceremonies, and even war. Civilization couldn't exist without play. He was one of the first to see play not just as a particular activity but rather as an aspect of all activities.

Jean Piaget

Mead and Huizinga were followed by Piaget, whose work is by far the most sophisticated theory of child's play and its serious function. Piaget, in his 1945 volume *Play, Dreams, and Imitation in Childhood*, theorized that infants begin playing by absorbing their environments.[12] During play, infants assimilate external reality into themselves through their senses. For the infant, play is entirely inward; external reality is internal reality. Playing with a ball or his mother is the same as playing with his fingers or voice. Consequently, play lacks differentiation, because it occurs entirely within the infant's own self-pleasuring, make-believe experience. The child's play is random, aimless, and without purposive intent. The child haphazardly plays for the pure pleasure of playing.

About age two, the child starts differentiating internal and external reality, although he still experiences "mommy" as his own internal reality. Piaget's work at this stage contradicts Claparede's idea that play is imitation. Because the child's experience remains undifferentiated, there is no one to playfully imitate. The functional value of this play is that the infant, whose body and brain are growing, slowly learns sensory and motor skills, which prepare him for meeting the challenges of external reality.

From ages two to seven, "playing play" gradually converts into playing games. Instead of merely assimilating, the child also accommodates to external reality. In addition to the "I am my play" of the first stage, the child now also realizes that "I play with something other than me." A ball is no longer merely something that the child soaks into himself. It also is something in itself and outside of himself, to which he adapts. In this stage the child plays practice games, by throwing and chasing a ball, like a kitten chasing a ball of yarn. Unlike the kitten that practices these "hunting" skills, the child plays with a ball for no apparent reason, other than as general practice or rehearsal for later development.

As the child's perceptual and motor skills continue developing, he readies himself for symbolic games. External and internal reality coalesce when the child grips the ball and imagines it to be an airplane, complete with sound effects. The ball is no longer just a ball, but also something else. By mastering this symbolic ability, he can represent the external object in his memory and imagination.

Soon, when he can't find his ball, he will hold up an open hand and roar "Varrooom," symbolizing his absent ball and representing a jet plane. Later, he will take this symbol a step further by becoming the noisy jet plane himself with winged arms buzzing birds and squirrels from the backyard. Next, the child will take sticks and string and construct his own toy jet. Piaget calls this a "constructional game," which builds on all the previous games and stages. Here the child continues accommodating to external reality by learning "rules." The rule that the child learns in our example is that one stick must cross another to match a fuselage with wings. External reality counterbalances internal reality; playing games offsets playing play during this accommodation stage.

Between eight and twelve, about the time when my grandfather welcomed me into the workforce, the play of symbolic and constructional games and play in general decline. *Gaming* displaces *playing*. Play ceases being important because it's no longer needed. The tadpole's tail drops off; it has done its job. Playing has served its function by preparing the child for the serious games of intellectual, work, and social life. In Piaget's view, the only play that persists into adulthood comes in the form of socialized games, which are controlled by rules that encourage important qualities in the functional adult, including discipline, organization, competition, and fairness.

Erik Erikson

Erik Erikson, like Piaget, had little need for the drama of Freud's hydraulics, strife, and compensatory function for understanding play. Although a psychoanalyst, Erikson didn't believe that play needed the fires of anxiety for its expression. In his 1950 work *Childhood and Society*, he explains play as a process that coaxes passage from one stage of development to the next, integrating each successive stage.[13] The challenges of everyday life present ample reason and opportunity to play without requiring the whistle of life's pressure cooker.

Erikson acknowledged the practical functions of play. Play provides the opportunity to experiment morally and to try out different realities. Children and adults encounter daily tasks and difficulties and plan and experiment with all sorts of methods and solutions. Mistakes are as valuable as successes in developing strategies and skills for the task of living life. Through the trial and error of play, we gather an increasingly complex assortment of skills and ideas, try them out, and discover masterful solutions. In other words, humans play naturally with problems and concerns and store their problem-solving experiences in an ever-expanding reservoir of creativity. Play prepares the child by helping her through development.

But Erikson's play opened a few gates in the growing field of play theory. First, he removes the lattice grating that confines play to childhood. He, like Freud, envisioned human experience as a doorless playhouse through which children and adults passed freely from cradle to grave, creating from their imaginations and dreams and mastering problems with an ever-growing repertoire of skills. While Piaget concentrated on play during childhood, Erikson saw play as a lifelong continuum.

Second, Erikson removes the practical adult, who, standing in the front doorway, insists that the occupants must have a function, a "why," for their play. Erikson writes, "To be tolerant of the child's play, the adult must invent theories which show either that childhood play is really work—or that it does not count" (214). For Erikson (like Huizinga), adults play too and, along with kids, they sometimes do it for the useless fun of it—which is why it is valuable. While Erikson believed that play functions to master new problems in new circumstances, he also noted that play is self-reinforcing, that is, it is driven for the "sheer delight" of the play itself. For him, play was not something to draw on when anxious or frustrated. Nor was it simply sports, recreation, leisure, games, and artistic expression. Rather, play is a basic human ability that grows and touches every facet of life, including work, thinking, and other serious activity. Erikson said that when we play, we "step sidewards into another reality," where we can safely explore and master problems which creates new possibilities for a more complex and integrated identity.[14]

Third, he opens all the doors to the outside and lets a breeze flow through. He realizes this playhouse is "another reality" into which we constantly sidestep. Erikson writes that play frees us from "the confinements of space and time and the definitiveness of social reality free from the compulsions of conscience and from the impulsions of irrationality."[15] It exists outside of space and time and social reality, between confinement and freedom, between the definite and the indefinite, and between rationality and irrationality.

Erikson would regard my Mickey Mouse fiasco as a playful experiment to creatively solve a problem by applying my drawing skill in a charming effort to appease my grandfather. Although a seeming failure, I deepened my understanding of others and enhanced my repertoire of problem-solving skills. I learned responsibility for cleaning up my mess, the importance of directly admitting my mistakes, and the common distinction between play and work. For Erikson, success and failure are part of the ongoing play that redeems the past and strengthens the hope for the future.

Donald Winnicott

Donald Winnicott was a British pediatrician and psychoanalyst who spent his entire life curious about play, especially the play of small children. Eulogized as a man whose entire life is best understood for his "capacity to play," Winnicott believed that playing is "a basic form of living."[16]

Winnicott's play theory is intriguing because he, like Erikson, locates play as another reality, as a threshold or *liminal* world, between the child's internal reality and his external environment, and often at the intersection of the child and another playmate, child or adult. Fascinated with Rabindranath Tagore's poem "On the Seashore," he adopted the seashore metaphor as the basis of his theory. In his 1971 book *Playing and Reality*, Winnicott described play's location as a "playground," as an "area [that] is not inner psychic reality. It is outside the individual, but it is not the external world." Play is an "intermediate area," a "third area," a "potential space," a zone of creativity between child and parent, inclusive of, but belonging to neither.[17]

In this play zone, the child glows with preoccupation, similar to the intense concentration of an adult. This zone vibrates as a "to and fro process" between "the baby's potential to find and the mother's being herself, waiting to be found." If a "good enough mother" and baby can remain present to their playful interaction, the baby experiences magical and "omnipotent" control. For Winnicott, the content of the play is irrelevant; what matters is the play process itself. As the baby repeatedly plays and feels this control, he experiences increasing safety, a harmony between internal and external reality, a bond with his parent, and, as Erikson asserts as well, the beginning of trust in his "identity-formation."

This playground is a process that pulsates between activity and rest, between overstimulation and understimulation, and between the anxiety of risk and the assurance of safety. It is also a third reality, a seashore between the internal and external reality, between confidence and uncertainty, and between the potential and the actual of development.

Unlike Freud's emphasis on the anxiety-ridden, intrapsychic play of the individual child, Winnicott views play as profoundly interpersonal. Play awakens gently in the "magic" of a "reliable intimacy" between people. Play flows back and forth as a mutually shared and deeply relational experience. As the ball of play rolls back and forth between parent and child, each influences and is influenced by this play. This initial play experience is the undifferentiated prototype for all future relationships, their conflicts, surprises, disappointments, and their joys. At its best, child and parent seem consumed in the ecstasy of play's harmonious flow. Call it love or play, they go to a "third world" and feel jarred and impatient when external reality intrudes and calls them back.

This primal play experience permits the next stage: the child's "being alone in the presence of someone." This means that the child can now comfortably play alone, because of the trust that grew from this initial play experience. The child trusts that the mother figure is psychologically present, although forgotten or physically absent, because she has become reliable and continues to be available in the baby's experience.

In the next stage, the baby gradually experiences a difference between himself and his parent. The parent introduces her own playing and discovers that her baby may like or dislike the play that is not his own. As differentiation continues and unfolds with increasing complexity, "the way is paved for a playing together in a relationship."[18]

Winnicott explored this seashore world of play further. A key concept was play as *transitional,* which refers to both the dynamic, to-and-fro process between the child's intrapsychic and external realities and the intermediate impetus for the child's movement from earlier to later stages. The transitional nature of play could be seen in several aspects: transitional objects, transitional phenomena, and transitional language.

A child's *transitional objects* are the first toys to which the infant becomes attached, like a soft blanket, a doll, or teddy bear. These objects, often held when falling asleep, going on a trip, or encountering the unfamiliar, are primitive symbols representing the infant's attachment to the mother figure. With these toys, the child creates a helpful illusion of her physical presence. They bridge the child's inner and outer reality and soften his separation during normal development. Often, the child appropriately prefers this toy to his mother, because it provides a sense of individuality, while remaining symbolically connected.

The child forms a similar attachment to *transitional phenomena,* such as mannerisms, rituals, images, and fantasies. The child might hug, kiss, and wave goodbye or have his back or face stroked before falling asleep. He might suck his thumb when meeting a stranger or imagine sucking his mother's breast.

This same process occurs with *transitional language*. From grunts and coos, the child moves to words and sentences. An overlay of all three "transitionals" would be observed when the child holds his teddy bear, waves, and says "bye-bye." Like his toys, transitional phenomena and language span internal and external reality and escort the child down the path of differentiation, yet within the safety of attachment.

Winnicott understood that this transitional play was not limited to children. In language, art, ritual, ceremony, literature, and poetry, he saw humankind reaching in and reaching out to connect with this in-between, third world of play. He understood that grown men and women have their religious symbols, talismans, photographs, gifts, and mementos that crystallized a present, meaningful connection that vibrates between internal and external reality, danger and safety, the potential and the actual, past failure and future possibility, the seen and the hidden, and the "no longer" and "not yet."

Eugen Fink

Eugen Fink was a philosopher, a phenomenologist closely associated with Heidegger and Husserl. In his 1960 volume *Play as Symbol of the World,* Fink both extended and revised many of Huizinga's ideas on play.[19] While Huizinga viewed play as separate and contrary to reality and its seriousness, monotonous labor, dry rationality, and claims of authenticity and superiority, Fink saw play as just another existential phenomenon along with work, death, love, and power. Fink's view regarding play's uniqueness is that play can absorb and re-present these phenomenon. "We play at being serious, we play truth, we play reality, we play work, we play love and death, and we even play play itself."[20]

Although Fink's preoccupations were deeply philosophical and less focused on everyday play, his correlation of child's play to "cosmic play" is a fascinating idea. Other theorists acknowledge the existence of play into adulthood but Fink sees our entire attempt to grasp the nature of the world as an extended type of play. Here, play is a *method* of understanding existence.[21]

PLAY AND PSYCHOLOGICAL DEVELOPMENT

The more we study play, the more crucial and serious this most "unserious" appearing of activities seems to be. Modern research has provided a treasure trove of empirical evidence that backs up what the great developmental thinkers proposed: that play is serious business and affects not just children but all of society. In their landmark 2009 volume *Play: How It Shapes the Brain, Opens the Imagination, and Invigorates the Soul,* Stuart Brown and Christopher Vaughn expound on a lifetime of research on the benefits of play. They find play to be a universal, biologically based instinct that humans need to survive and thrive.

The importance of play for psychological health is evident in so many areas of study, from my own private therapy practice to studies of some of the most harrowing human behaviors we know.

Play and Psychotherapy

All of these aspects of play weave in and out of my work as a psychotherapist. Indeed, psychotherapy is one of the professions that have looked to play as a means to solve problems and imagine opportunities in our work. Plato and Aristotle would smile approvingly when we "think outside of the box," role-play customer relations, test out military scenarios with war games, and imagine pitfalls and possibilities. Daily, we recruit play in the service of serious work.

I've seen the value of this in my own work as a psychotherapist. Besides coaxing clients to think through their predicaments, therapists invite them to play by imagining themselves and their relationships in novel ways. They invite clients to picture "writing" the next chapters and the conclusion to their life's "book" and to imagine metaphors about men from Mars and women from Venus. They offer role plays with twists and reversals that loosen their pathos, plumb the depths of their psyches, and envision creative alternatives.

An example of the value of playing in psychotherapy was a client of mine named Marta, who had started therapy after her husband Hank had an affair. The two had experienced some success with a marital therapist, and Marta reported that Hank had shown a sincere effort to improve their marriage. But Marta came to me because she still felt depressed, disinterested in sex, and responsible for her marriage's paralysis. Her self-blame only magnified her gloom. Medication helped, as did journal writing, reading self-help books, and going to seminars. But Marta said she still felt "flat and colorless."

I asked Marta if she would be willing to play with her struggle. I had learned that she was a skilled public speaker and asked if she would pretend giving an extemporaneous speech to an audience of male philanderers. Her topic was "How Men's Affairs Affect Their Wives." Marta balked at first, but as she started to talk, she became more and more animated. She found herself using the word "punish," both in reference to how men's affairs punish their wives and how wives punish themselves for their husband's affairs. Noting this, I then asked her to deliver a speech to an imaginary group of wives who felt guilty for their husbands' affairs. Marta easily went through how women take unhealthy responsibility for their husband's bad behavior. While exhorting her imaginary audience to "take responsibility for yourself," she paused, quietly mumbled "But that's easier said than done," and began to cry.

When she recovered, she said that she felt stuck and couldn't go on. I asked her to sit in the "audience" chair and invite another playmate to our drama. I asked her to choose a woman whom she admired to speak next to the audience. Marta quickly picked Marianne, a psychologist and author whom she had read and heard speak at a seminar. I asked Marta to close her eyes and listen to Marianne's speech. Reviewing the talk in her mind, she remembered Marianne saying that we need to forgive ourselves before we can truly forgive anyone else.

At this point, I pushed Marta further, suggesting a fictitious meeting between her and Marianne. I posed that Marianne knew everything thus far and that they pretend to dialogue with this in mind. Marta shuttled back and forth from her chair to the imaginary Marianne's chair, as she enacted the dialogue:

Marta (M): "I'm stuck. I know I need to take responsibility for myself. I know that I need to forgive myself before I can really let the affair go and forgive Hank. But I can't seem to do it no matter how hard I try." (Moves to Marianne's chair)

Marta as Marianne (M as M): "It's tough. Maybe you're still pissed off at Hank."

M: "Damn right, I AM still mad."

M as M: "So you still need to punish him?"

M: "Yea." (Smiling a devilish smile)

I introject here: "Add the phrase, 'and there is a part of me that likes punishing him.'"

M: (Animated, smiling) "Yea, there's a part of me that likes it."

M as M: "Feels good."

M (embarrassed yet animated): "Yeah, I like the power, the control! I like jerking Hank around."

M as M: "Like a choke leash. He'd run off and mount some bitch if you don't keep a tight grip."
M (now very energized): "Yeah, if I punish and choke the bastard, he'll walk the line." (Laughs)
M as M: "Guess you don't trust him. Better to control him than trust him, right?"
M (nodding in silence, tears well in her eyes, she begins to sob): "What a bitch I am!"
M as M: "As long as you punish him, you punish you. As long as you keep jerking his chain, you won't get hurt; you don't have to trust him. But the other side is you can't love doing this. Neat game, Marta! Kinda fun, up to a point."
M (out of role and lighthearted): "I get it. This game's no fun anymore."

How do we view Marta's session relative to serious work and play? Do we take Aristotle's idea and say that a separate and subordinate play served the serious and more important work of the overall therapy? Do we take a Freudian perspective and state that play provided an escape valve for her unconscious fear and rage so the primary work of analysis could finally occur? Do we echo Erikson and assert that Marta's play was equal to her hard, thoughtful work and together they helped her creatively examine and solve her problem? Or do we say that the session suggests that play, not the serious work of analysis, was superior, since it most directly led to Marta's resolution?

As I reflected on the session, I felt that, just as travel opens our eyes to the world or seeing a great work of art in person reveals something new in the artwork, play allows what was hidden in plain sight to emerge clearly. The logical, thoughtful work that came before was like a low rung on a ladder, one that got her going. But logical analysis and critical thinking went only so far in soothing the soul's suffering. It was Marta's ability to indulge in playfulness that unleashed something new and powerful that allowed her to heal.

Lack of Play and Aggression

If my own practice supports the healthy contributions of play, many researchers prove the dire consequences when it's missing. In her 2009 article "The Serious Need for Play," Melinda Wenner summarizes much of the recent research on everyday play. She begins by telling the story behind a psychiatrist named Stuart Brown's research:

> On August 1, 1966, the day psychiatrist Stuart Brown started his assistant professorship at the Baylor College of Medicine in Houston, 25-year-old Charles Whitman climbed to the top of the University of Texas Tower on the Austin campus and shot 46 people. Whitman, an engineering student and a former U.S. Marine sharpshooter, was the last person anyone expected to go on a killing spree. After Brown was assigned as the state's consulting psychiatrist

to investigate the incident and later, when he interviewed 26 convicted Texas murderers for a small pilot study, he discovered that most of the killers, including Whitman, shared two things in common: they were from abusive families, and they never played as kids.[22]

Wenner concludes: "A handful of studies support Brown's conviction that a play-deprived childhood disrupts normal social, emotional and cognitive development in humans and animals. He and other psychologists worry that limiting free play in kids may result in a generation of anxious, unhappy and socially maladjusted adults."

Wenner cites other researchers who have discovered important insights about play, like educational psychologist Anthony Pellegrini, noting that play teaches social skills. "'You don't become socially competent via teachers telling you how to behave,' Pellegrini says, 'You learn [social] skills by interacting with your peers, learning what's acceptable, what's not acceptable.' Children learn to be fair and take turns—they cannot always demand to be the fairy queen, or soon they have no playmates. 'They want this thing to keep going, so they're willing to go the extra mile to accommodate others' desires,' he explains. Because kids enjoy the activity, they do not give up as easily in the face of frustration as they might on, say, a math problem—which helps them develop persistence and negotiating abilities." And play turns out to be the context in which children employ their most sophisticated language skills.

The lack of play can be devastating for children's development. Wenner cites a 1997 study of children living in poverty by the HighScope Educational Research Foundation that found that "kids who enrolled in play-oriented preschools are more socially adjusted later in life than are kids who attended play-free preschools where they were constantly instructed by teachers. By age twenty-three, more than one-third of kids who had attended instruction-oriented preschools had been arrested for a felony as compared with fewer than one-tenth of the kids who had been in play-oriented preschools. And as adults, fewer than 7 percent of the play-oriented preschool attendees had ever been suspended from work, but more than a quarter of the directly instructed kids had."

Science writer Bryant Furlow found the same evidence for play's role in development.[23] He noted that in primates, "the amount the brain grows between birth and maturity reflects the amount of play in which each species engages." In neuroimaging studies, play "lights everything up." Play may have a role in synapse retention, since it appears that early in life, synapses that are not activated end up getting "culled."

The research is chock full of empirical studies demonstrating the critical benefits of play. It seems that play is woven into our very natures—one more reason why play may be the perfect vehicle and metaphor for our most profound human journeys and spiritual aspirations.

CONCLUSION

Fascination with the phenomenon of play cuts across time and disciplines. My own interest in play blossomed in the 1960s. One day in 1963, while perusing my Catholic college's library, I flipped open Nietzsche's *The Joyful Wisdom* and found this: "Another idea runs on before us, a strange, tempting ideal, full of danger, to which we should not wish to persuade anyone, because we do not readily concede the right to it to anyone: the ideal of *a spirit who plays* naively (that is to say involuntarily and from overflowing abundance and power) with everything that has been previously been called holy, good, inviolable, divine" (emphasis added).[24]

When I visited my philosophy professor, he quickly pigeonholed Nietzsche as the "ultimate blasphemer" who touted the spirit of willful supermen, not the Divine Spirit. After telling him about my early experience with Sister Fabian, he smiled and opened the *Enneads*, the work of the third-century Neoplatonic mystic Plotinus. He read, "Making play to begin with before taking up the subject seriously, we affirm: All things strive toward *theoria*, the vision of God. Does that mean that this treatise of mine is itself nothing but a kind of game? For, after all, things that play, play only because of their urge to attain a vision of God, whether they are the seriousness of a grown man, or the play of the child."[25] He explained that Nietzsche and Plotinus had a similar take on the possibilities of spirited play, but they pursued very different directions. Nietzsche's play focused on its power in the human spirit, while Plotinus's play stretched to the Divine Spirit. He directed me to the more orthodox ideas about play in Plato, Aristotle, and St. Thomas Aquinas. Then he generously gave me his extra copy of Johann Huizinga's classic *Homo Ludens* (Man, the Player). I wondered how such opposite views could come from the same idea.

With priests and nuns dotting my family's genealogical landscape, I followed this familiar road into the seminary to study for the priesthood. In the late 1960s and early 1970s, there was an explosion of Christian theological interest in play. I learned about the play of Wisdom in Proverbs 8 and more about Jesus's directive to "become as little children." I delighted in the play ideas from the theological works of saints Gregory Nazianzus and Maximus the Confessor and the Jesuit Hugo Rahner. I read the play theologies and thoughts of Jurgen Moltmann, Hans von Baltazar, David Miller, Robert Neale, and Martin Buber.

When I left the seminary for graduate training in psychology, my interest in play took a secular turn. But there is no doubt about the importance of play to mystics and theologians and philosophers through the ages. Modern science has only confirmed the instincts of ancients. We now know that through play children learn how to manage conflict and solve problems because they want to have fun, which requires getting along with their playmates. Even when kids play alone in unstructured situations, the intrinsic optimism of their play imagines how things can turn out well. There is also evidence that play nudges a child's neural growth and snips away unnecessary neurological processes, thereby encouraging higher brain functioning and language development. Play seems crucial for promoting creative, socially adjusted, and bright children.[26]

Whereas play forms children, it soothes adults. It relaxes us and encourages joy and creativity. Adult play shines in the expression of art and curiosity-driven science. But adults must navigate the tricky waters between play and social order. Play above all presents us with possibilities—and learning to embrace that power without abusing it is one of the keys to play.

NOTES

1. Maurie Backman, "Here's a New Reason to Work Fewer Hours," *The Motley Fool*, June 14, 2017.

2. Abigail Hess, "Here's How Many Paid Vacation Days the Typical American Worker Gets," *CNBC.com*, July 6, 2018.

3. Bryan Robinson, "Chained to the Desk," *Family Therapy Networker* 24, no. 4 (2000): 29.

4. Cited in David Miller, *God and Games* (New York: World Publishing, 1969), 108.

5. Cited in Karl Groos, *The Play of Man*, trans. E. Baldwin (New York: Appleton, 1901), 398–399.

6. Plato, *Laws I* (643C), *Republic IV* (424), *Republic* (537).

7. Edouard Claparede, *Experimental Pedagogy and the Psychology of the Child* (London: Edward Arnold, 1911). See also Susanna Millar, *The Psychology of Play* (New York: Jason Aronson, 1974), 13–22, for additional history about nineteenth- and early twentieth-century psychological thought about play.

8. Cindy Aron, *Working at Play* (Oxford: Oxford University Press, 1999).

9. Sigmund Freud, *Beyond the Pleasure Principle* (New York: Liveright, 1961).

10. Sigmund Freud, *On Creativity and the Unconscious* (New York: Harper and Row Torchbooks, 1958).

11. George Herbert Mead, *Mind, Self, and Society* (Chicago: University of Chicago Press, 1934).

12. Jean Piaget, *Play, Dreams, and Imitation in Childhood*, trans. C. Gattegno and F. Hodgson (New York: Norton, 1951).

13. Erik Erikson, *Childhood and Society* (New York: Norton, 1950).

14. Erikson, *Childhood and Society*, 209–238.

15. Erikson, *Childhood and Society*, 214.

16. Simon Grolnick and L. Barkin (eds.), *Between Reality and Fantasy* (Northvale, NJ: Aronson, 1988), 18.

17. Donald Winnicott, *Playing and Reality* (New York: Basic Books, 1971), 47–52.

18. Winnicott, *Playing and Reality*, 47–52.

19. Eugen Fink, *Play as Symbol of the World and Other Writings*, trans. Alexander Moore and Christopher Turner (Bloomington: Indiana University Press, 2016).

20. Eugen Fink, Ute Saine, and Thomas Saine, "The Oasis of Happiness: Toward an Ontology of Play," *Yale French Studies* 41, Game, Play, Literature (1968): 19–30.

21. Fink et al., "Oasis of Happiness," 22.

22. Melinda Wenner, "The Serious Need for Play," *Scientific American*, February 2009.

23. Bryant Furlow, "Play's the Thing," *New Scientist* magazine, June 9, 2001, https://www.newscientist.com/article/mg17022944-600-plays-the-thing/

24. Friedrich Nietzsche, *The Joyful Wisdom*, trans. T. Common (New York: Frederick Ungar, 1960), 352. This work has also been published under the title *The Gay Science*.

25. Plotinus, *Enneads*, III, 8, 1.

26. Wenner, "The Serious Need for Play."

Chapter 2

Possibility Play

> Ballad by the Fire
> Life is the game that must be played:
> This truth at least, good friend, we know;
> So live and laugh, nor be dismayed
> As one by one the phantoms go.
>
> —Edwin Arlington Robinson

Long before he was a world-renowned poet, Edwin Arlington Robinson was a child in an unhappy family hobbled by neglect and alcoholism. His parents failed to give him a name until a concerned vacationer from Arlington, Massachusetts, drew "Edwin" from a hat and proposed it to Robinson's father. His father died early, requiring Edwin to leave school and tend his family's farm. His brother Herman slowly drank himself to death. He proposed marriage twice and was turned down both times. And when he finally gathered the means to self-publish his first book, his mother, to whom the volume was dedicated, died three days before the book was published.

Robinson had a hard life, but he found ways to survive. His poetry and his friendships were like sparks from a campfire on a dark night. When Teddy Roosevelt's son read his poetry and recommended it to his father, Robinson's career caught fire. He received the Pulitzer Prize for Poetry in 1922, 1925, and 1928.

E. A. Robinson wrote at a time between the dusk of idealism and the dawn of materialistic determinism, between the cheerfulness of the Romantics and the gloomy demands of the industrial age. Play in the usual jolly sense was easy for the Romantics. In 1795 Friedrich Schiller famously said, "Man plays only when he is, in the full sense of the word, a man, and he is only wholly man when he is playing." He also wrote, "It is only through Beauty that man makes his way to Freedom"—sharing with countless other Romantics the belief that gratifying the play instinct was a means to reaching higher realms.[1] But jolly play was not an option for Robinson. He recognized that we are compelled to run on the path that we are given and must make of that journey what we will. He had no use for the play of the privileged and happy. He wanted to take play into the dismal place where he actually lived.

Robinson wrote that we *must* play, that we are fated to play. He saw that we are thrown into this world like a roll of fate's dice. Whether we are sevens or snake eyes depends on chance, which decides our socioeconomic, political, environmental, religious, and cultural circumstances as children. We cannot choose our parents nor our genetic makeup. As children, we are either privileged, poor, or somewhere in between. Even as adults, these circumstances have a powerful sway on our lives.

While the previous chapter on everyday play focused on what play does for us developmentally, this chapter looks at play as a worldview, how great thinkers throughout history have considered it a symbol representing the freedom that we are able to exercise within the confines of our own circumstances, a model for creativity, and a metaphor for engaging with life's uncertainties. All of these cases exemplify play as *possibility*.

PLAY AS FREEDOM

For Robinson and others, playing meant making choices within whatever context we find ourselves. Robinson's view of fate was not to compete with or submit to it but to embrace it (an early variation, perhaps, of the refusal to try to dominate our impulses and circumstances that thinkers like Dewey and James advocated, discussed in chapter 4). To play with fate meant making choices within the rules of the game. In this paradigm, play is first and foremost a metaphor for *freedom*.

The Stoics: Epictetus

As we will see, the existentialists are famous for making freedom the center of their philosophy. But they were far from the first to contemplate personal choice amid impersonal circumstances—nor to touch on play as a central metaphor. The Stoic philosopher Epictetus lived in the first and second centuries CE in Rome and later Greece. His lecture notes were gathered by a pupil named Arrian and compiled in the *Discourses*.[2]

In the *Discourses* Epictetus encourages his students to appreciate that external things are indifferent, being neither good nor bad. With this in mind, we should imitate those who play dice, for neither the dice nor the counters have any real value; what matters, and what is either good or bad, is the way we play the game. Later, Epictetus discusses the example of playing a ball game.[3] No one considers for a moment whether the ball itself is good or bad, but only whether they can throw and catch it with the appropriate skill. What matters are the faculties of dexterity, speed, and good judgment exhibited by the players, for it is in deploying these faculties effectively that any player is deemed to have played well.

Epictetus distinguished between things in our power (*prohairetic* things, to use his technical term) and things not in our power (*aprohairetic* things). Aprohairetic things are our circumstances, our parents, and the weather. So we must disregard them and concentrate on prohairetic things: "That alone is in our power, which is our own work; and in this class are our opinions, impulses, desires, and aversions. What, on the contrary, is not in our power, are our bodies, possessions, glory, and power. Any delusion on this point leads to the greatest errors, misfortunes, and troubles, and to the slavery of the soul."[4]

Epictetus knew of what he spoke. He spent his youth as a slave in Rome, and the very name Epictetus means "acquired." It's speculated that he was crippled because his owner broke his leg deliberately. He knew the difference between slavery of the body and slavery of the soul. Epictetus urges us to "remember who we are" and what "name" we have, because what role we play in life will determine which actions are appropriate for us. This also brings in the notion of our having to accept our fate, whatever that may be, since we do not ourselves chose the role we must play; for although we may aim for one role rather than another, we must recognize that our attaining it is not, in fact, "in our power." He writes, "Remember that you are an actor in a play, which is as the author [i.e., God] wants it to be: short, if he wants it to be short; long, if he wants it to be long. If he wants you to act a poor man, a cripple, a public official, or a private person, see that you act it with skill. For it is your job to act well the part that is assigned to you; but to choose it is another's."[5]

His belief in the absolute freedom of the individual led him even to sanction suicide. He uses the metaphor of playing games when discussing suicide, for just as someone stops playing a game when they are no longer amused by it, so it should be in life generally: If life should become unbearable, no one can force us to keep living it. He writes, "Remember that the door is open. Do not be more cowardly than children, but just as they say, when the game no longer pleases them, 'I will play no more,' you too, when things seem that way to you, should merely say, 'I will play no more,' and so depart; but if you stay, stop moaning."[6]

Epictetus extended his play metaphor to the image of an athlete exercising in preparation for the Olympic Games:

Therefore take the decision right now that you must live as a full-grown man, as a man who is making progress; and all that appears to be best must be to you a law that cannot be transgressed. And if you are confronted with a hard task or with something pleasant, or with something held in high repute or no repute, remember *that the contest is now, and that the Olympic games are now,* and that it is no longer possible to delay the match, and that progress is lost and saved as a result of one defeat and even one moment of giving in.[7] (Emphasis added)

Heraclitus: The Ancient Postmodernist

Epictetus belonged to the philosophical school known as Stoics, and a notable inspiration for the Stoics was the much earlier Greek/Ionian philosopher Heraclitus. Heraclitus was born into a royal family in Ionia in the sixth century BCE and is rumored to have spent his days playing knucklebones in the Temple of Artemis; when he was asked to assume his duties as a lawmaker, he replied that he found the law tiresome. A lifelong misanthrope, Heraclitus tended toward negativity and was known as the Weeping Philosopher. One well-known quote demonstrates his doom-and-gloom view: "The fairest universe is but a heap of rubbish piled up at random."[8]

Although Heraclitus did not delight in the notion of life as play as Epictetus did, he nonetheless paid tribute to the variable, superficial, and gamelike nature of the universe. He railed against those who simply believed as others told them to believe—"human opinions are children's toys"[9] (harkening toward an "as if" mentality of later thinkers)—and acknowledged a kind of perverse triviality in reality—"Eternity is a child moving counters in a game; the kingly power is a child's."[10] He believed that steady principles like justice were understood only by the gods and tipped his hat at the inconstancy of the universe. His famous dictum "You cannot step into the same stream twice" acknowledged the transitory and slippery ground rules of life.

The critic Mihai Spariosu wrote of this ancient worldview: "Zeus scatters good and evil fates or lots among men not according to any principle of fair play, let alone divine justice, but according to his whims."[11] For Spariosu, the play metaphor is key: The Homeric cosmos is "not so much like a piece of clockwork as it is like a game of celestial snakes and ladders. Most moves are free; but should one alight at the foot of one's particular ladder, or at the head of one particular snake, the next move is determined."[12]

The Existentialists

Freedom was perhaps most deeply contemplated by the existentialists. Early thinkers associated with existentialism include Soren Kierkegaard and Friedrich Nietzsche in the nineteenth century. They were some of the first Europeans to live in an intellectual society in which the traditional notions of

Christianity—and indeed all religions—had lost currency. But they viewed nothingness as offering humans freedom and possibility rather than despair. Heidegger proposed facing the dreadful nothingness of death (life-unto-death) as the beginning of living an authentic, freely chosen life.

These nineteenth-century thinkers initiated much of existential thought, but it was in the twentieth century, especially after World War II, that existentialism really blossomed. Its core concepts included the famed maxim "existence before essence" (meaning we are what we do, not how we mentally categorize ourselves); the objective meaninglessness of the universe encapsulated in the term "absurd"; our responsibility to create our own lives; and the primacy of feeling and meaning over rationality. These ideas were elaborated by philosophers such as Jean-Paul Sartre, Simone de Beauvoir, and Albert Camus.

One of the most powerful thinkers in this regard was Victor Frankl. Frankl was a Jewish psychologist who was tortured and starved in German concentration camps during World War II. Holocaust survivors tend to speak with a bottom-line authority. They are stripped of almost all outward choice and experience horrific things. But Frankl realized that, with only two cards to play in the otherwise empty deck of a Nazi concentration camp, he still could trump madness and hatred with the aces of freedom and love. As he famously wrote in his book *Man's Search for Meaning*, "Everything can be taken from a man but one thing: the last of the human freedoms—to choose one's attitude in any given set of circumstances, to choose one's own way."[13]

In a dehumanizing atmosphere that led many to acts of horror and selfishness, Frankl led his life as if the outward circumstances had no effect on him. He wrote, "It did not really matter what we expected from life, but rather what life expected from us. We needed to stop asking about the meaning of life, and instead to think of ourselves as those who were being questioned by life—daily and hourly. Our answer must consist, not in talk and meditation, but in right action and in right conduct." And so he lived in Auschwitz. He shared a precious potato with a dying comrade, offered therapy to fellow prisoners, and worked relentlessly for the good of others.

Few of us possess Frankl's heroism. But we all face the same dilemma: Life provides the field, and we play on it. We can whine on the sidelines, strike out at others, and try to run scared. Or we can engage fully with the players on the field and the equipment we've been given. Frankl noted that we can't pursue success; we can only pursue right living, and success may follow.

PLAY AS CREATIVITY

If freedom emphasizes our moral choices, play as creativity (or imagination, as we termed it in the introduction) opens the door to "what if" scenarios that allow us to roam among unrealized worlds and ideas. This is inherently joyful but also allows us to see more, feel more, understand and empathize more—and perhaps solve more. Troy Camplin writes of this aspect of play in the work of critic Mihai Spariosu:

> Spariosu's ideas on the role of play . . . can help us better understand . . . postmodern views on art, literature, and culture. Spariosu sees literature as acting in what he calls a "ludic-liminal" manner—play—and on the threshold of perception. He sees literature (I would include all of the arts) as a form of play that challenges our perceptions, and can result in our changing the very world we live in. It does not attempt to do this through the exercise of power (as the postmodernists would have us believe), but through presenting us with "what if" scenarios we can either accept or reject.[14]

Camplin notes that "ideal readers will not attempt to master the text or enter into a competitive relation with it. On the contrary, they will approach it in a 'spirit of responsive understanding, opening themselves to it and allowing themselves to experience, through it, that liminal time-space which can produce alternative realities and new historical worlds'" (Spariosu, 228). A reader (and critic) must enter into the author's play-space, not sit on the sidelines and merely critique.

Play consultant Pat Kane's motto is "Play will be to the 21st century what work was to the industrial age—the dominant way of knowing, doing, and creating value." Kane helps companies and organizations around the world use play to open up creative possibilities for their enterprises. On his blog *The Play Ethic*, Kane talks at length about play as possibility, referencing the philosopher Schiller and the cultural critic Terry Eagleton:

> In *The Ideology of the Aesthetic*, Terry Eagleton devotes a chapter to Schiller's *Letters on the Aesthetic Education of Man,* one of the most important theories of play ever developed. The "play-drive" for Schiller is the ground of possibility of all human action: it suspends the destructive tendencies both of our appetites (sense-drive) and our reason (form-drive) and creates a zone of "free determinability." From this sublime experience of possible states of being (which Schiller terms "aesthetic"), we will be able to assess the best, most "graceful" options for personal and social action.
>
> Eagleton notes that Schiller's evocation of the importance of play allowed Marx to envision the kind of rich, fully extended humanity that exploitation and alienation would damage and distort. "Marx's critique of industrial capitalism is deeply rooted in a Schillerian vision of stunted capacities [and] dissociated powers."[15]

If this all sounds a little too high-flown for a tech blog, Kane brings the question down to earth. Play has "consequences for how we arrange our productive lives":

At the very least, one can point to the amazing diversity on this list—every "adaptive potentiation" from a mark-up language that encodes the working conditions of its sites, to an iPhone app that helps you do voluntary info-work for charities, to Ned Rossiter's "organised networks" as the successor to trade unions—as indication that an extraordinary creative energy is being tapped. Shirky tells us that it's a matter of insanely-easy group-forming networks opening up space beneath the Coasian floor, but there's more to it than that. To explain this fecundity, I [turn] to what has to be called . . . the "socio-biology" of play . . . [whose] playgrounds have 1) loose but robust governance, 2) ensure a surplus of time, space and stuff, [and] 3) treat failure, risk and mess as developmental necessities.[16]

Creativity is one of our greatest urges and greatest joys. But critique and fear of failure can shut it down—not just aesthetic criticism but even moral criticism if too hemmed in by convention. Choices are not just right and wrong; they are also interesting, curious, and opening to possibility. We have to suspend notions of good and bad, at least for a time, because this bifurcation is the quickest way to eliminate creative potential. We must entertain the options in that "in-between" place of play beyond right and wrong, tried and true.[17] It is on Kane's playgrounds that we will thrive, invent, and solve.

ENGAGING WITH UNCERTAINTY: PLAYING "AS IF" WITH GOD

Troy Camplin writes of Spariosu's idea that art presents us "with 'what if' scenarios we can either accept or reject." Spariosu intuits something very close to Schiller's play-drive, a turning away from competitiveness and instead "opening [ourselves] to . . . alternative realities and new historical worlds."[18]

Looked at this way, it's not surprising that one of the most fecund areas of possibility play is theology. As discussed in the introduction, in the modern age we often feel torn between the false certainties of traditional religions and the hollowness of a fractured postmodernism that destroys the grand narratives of the past but offers little in return. Choosing among these options, we end up as cynics or fundamentalists or dabblers. As Richard Rohr stated, we will run toward anything "to flee this terrible cloud of unknowing."[19] Much of recent psychology has spotlighted how we try desperately to avoid uncomfortable states—and end up in worse ones. And a state of uncertainty—what Plato called aporia—can seem unbearable.

But what if uncertainty were seen through the lens of play? So much depends on our outlook. G. K. Chesterton once wrote, "An adventure is only an inconvenience rightly considered. An inconvenience is only an adventure wrongly considered."[20] What if we were able to experience uncertainty as play rather than paralysis? And play as uncertainty "rightly considered"?

Seeing theology as play works on several levels. First, it allows us to admit openly a truth that we often try to skirt: that ultimately every religion—every spiritual idea, in fact—is made up, is a speculative faith experience, and falls into the category of "as if." We propose that the world is a certain way, that God has certain characteristics, and that certain practices will take us from point A to point B on our spiritual journey. Investigation into the "as if" nature of our spiritual beliefs has a long pedigree. Back in the sixth century BCE, the pre-Socratic philosopher Xenophanes posited that, although truth or reality exists, humans cannot truly know it. We can only put forth working hypotheses and act accordingly.[21] More recent philosophers like Kant, Vaihinger, and Nietzsche thought similarly.

Admitting the "as if" nature of our theological ideas has several virtues: It is an exercise in humility, for one. Although God may be omnipotent and omniscient, we humans are not. It is all too easy to mistake God's perfection with our own and be carried away into treating our ideas and beliefs as facts.

It may also put the brakes on our most destructive instincts. If we admit that our beliefs are simply our best guesses as to the nature of the universe, we might be less inclined to punish others for disagreeing. This was roughly the point of view of Erasmus, a moderate soul caught in between the twin zealotries of the Reformation and its backlash. His *On Mending the Peace of the Church* and other writings urged Christians not to argue over doctrines that ultimately couldn't be affirmed with certainty—when to fast, when to baptize, how often (and to whom) one should confess. Keep it simple, he urged, and let others choose what they think is right for their own practice. The Catholic inquisitions and Protestant firebrands like Luther and Zwingli did not agree.

The world's religions differ in many ways, especially doctrinally. But if we put aside rigid doctrines, we find that, underneath their cosmologies and narratives and "shalls" and "shall nots," they all have at least one thing in common: the goal of transcending selfishness—sometimes called "ego-transformation." Spirituality is, in essence, the quest for ego-transformation. A spiritual person is one who has a generosity of spirit, who is capable of self-sacrifice, who lives in peace and joy, and who has something outside of himself that is more important than him. Ultimately what matters is not how rational a belief is or how "right" a religion is; what matters is what our spiritual practices do in terms of ego-transformation. We cannot know if our beliefs are true, but we can know whether they are helpful, whether acting as if they are true is a useful way to live.

GOD'S OWN "AS IF"

Heraclitus's famous dictum that we never step in the same stream twice has interesting echoes in the postmodern distrust and eternals, the very starting point for so much contemporary philosophy. It equally echoes the play of nature that contemporary scientists have found in the fields of evolution and physics. Many thinkers have taken the scientific discoveries of the twentieth and twenty-first centuries as a kind of new cosmology—clues that point us to a truer conception of reality than the old stories and mythologies. But even those who hold to traditional forms of religion may find within the realities of modern physics odd but compelling ideas to incorporate into those traditional forms. Science becomes *part* of our spiritual explorations, not just a set of facts lying beside them.

So what are the characteristics of modern science that thinkers have found so inspiring? For one, the scientific discoveries of the modern era are replete with the characteristics of play. They are both relational and interactional and have adaptive variability, flexibility, redundancy (in junk genes, for example), and diversity. They follow unpredictable, quirky courses and have hidden, latent potentials, surprising interactions, and inherent uncertainty. Morphogenesis, the collective memory of species, recalls the feeling of being "in sync" with another teammate, band member, or dance partner. Complexity theorists talk of the spontaneous emergence of evolution and new levels of self-organization that permit further evolving.

And while both evolution and play seem to proceed with increasing complexity—from random, purposeless, and chaotic processes to structure, pattern, purpose, and order—there is not necessarily a determined order or any specific end. Evolution evolves—and play plays—with no particular guidance, plan, direction, or rules. There is an aspect of amorality to both that can evoke a queasy feeling because the process remains uncertain, even arbitrary, even as what humans do within that process may be good or bad. Modern scientists seem to call back to the ancient philosophy of Lucretius, who saw the world as nothing but atoms, zinging around the universe without a GPS or a road map, yet still creating, through their swerves and collisions, the world we have.

This evolution is not just physical or taxonomic. The German philosopher Georg Hegel (1770–1831) wrote of the "Spirit" of world history unfolding toward self-realization. For Hegel, Spirit worked its way through all different cultures and civilizations, "jumping from place to place" in the world, now through monarchies, now through democracies. For Hegel this upward movement from one expression to another is in terms of increasing *freedom*. Freedom moves from one person (e.g., a king or tyrant) to the many (democratic societies). Hegel includes constraint as part of freedom because freedom necessitates its own opposite—otherwise it would become chaotic anarchy or negative freedom and consequently undermine freedom itself. Freedom and necessity (in the sense of constraint) act in a dynamic tension to give a synthesis of a new, more durable and universal freedom. Hegel's Spirit carried with it a sense of purpose that is more related to ideas about intelligent design than chaos theory, but his dialecticism and imagery of a Spirit jumping from one place and time to another, manifesting itself diversely, touches on something of this playful, undetermined development of the world.

Many other approaches to evolution include the acknowledgment of some spiritual force that initiated a purposeful unfolding of creation into the future. In some circles this purposefulness suggests that there is a personal God who has a plan that culminates in a better world, a tenet of what is sometimes called intelligent design. Though intelligent design is often derided as a gussied-up version of creation science, this "argument from design" for God's existence without a doubt offers a playful take on God's plan, visible in everything from the Fibonacci sequence to the platypus bill.

Others view God's initial creation as aimless, as a spontaneous act without any particular direction or plan. In this divine big bang, humanity is a quirky feature, part of an indeterminate spillage born of divine play. In this view, nothing is necessarily intended in the unfolding of the world, which because of its material and biological nature will decay. This creation is limited in time and space, is imperfect, is a walking, talking Murphy's Cosmic Law—something can and will go wrong. In this view of evolution as play, the world is a hit and miss, and at times catastrophic. But through our creativity—by embracing our capacity for action on God's field of play—we develop our capacity for altruism, compassion, kindness, and learning from mistakes. And through these virtues and talents, we can alter the playing field and make it better.

These scientific accounts—or imaginings—of the world point not to our own spiritual playfulness but ultimately to God's. As we practice our "as ifs," so God seems to try out his own.

CONCLUSION

The metaphor of playing the game of life freely is both current and ancient. It is as old as Buddhism and Stoicism and as new as existentialism and postmodernism. Many of the thinkers discussed here felt uncertain about God, whether expressed as the inscrutability of Heraclitus' Zeus or the nothingness of Sartre. While this uncertainty can cause discomfort, it ultimately offers beautiful opportunities. We realize that the responsibility lies squarely on us to take care of one another in this life and to provide meaning. It's a reversal of Pascal's wager: It invites us to live as if there is no God and the only meaning and happiness is found in this life; and if there is a meaningful and happy God, chances are he will be pleased and reward us. Perhaps God doesn't want us to figure out his plan; maybe he wants us to play with our possibilities.

The possibilities inherent in play are both exhilarating and dangerous. We must all navigate the tricky waters between play and social order. Friedrich

Nietzsche believed in the freedom to create a world with its own rules, not to follow the herd mentality or be the plaything of forces beyond our control. The person who could create freely would be Nietzsche's famed *Ubermensch*, the free spirit, who casts off the adult conventions of behavior and becomes like a child in the pursuit of creative play: "The child is innocence and forgetting, a new beginning, a game, a self-propelled wheel, a first movement, a sacred 'Yes.' For the game of creation, my brothers, a sacred 'Yes' is needed: the spirit now wills his own will, and he who had been lost to the world now conquers the world."[22]

Nietzsche's detractors cite his emphasis on freedom over duty, but Nietzsche discards only conventional rules, not necessarily goodness. It's an important distinction, and one that remains blurry in Nietzsche's writings. Play—without the healthy brakes of restraint, self-control, and society—can tip into extravagance, self-indulgence, and fixation. It can teeter from speculation and imagination into deceit and irresponsibility. Likewise it can veer into dark realms of manipulation and power. This is where *play* becomes *game*—too often a field of ugly competition and the will to win. So before we can "play with" play as a path to God, we must first contend with play as a path to power and a deviation into darkness.

NOTES

1. Friedrich Schiller, *On the Aesthetic Education of a Man in a Series of Letters*, trans. Reginald Snell (New Haven, CT: Yale University Press, 1954; orig. 1795).

2. Epictetus, *Discourses*, 2.5.2, in *Discourses, Fragments, Handbook*, trans. Robin Hard (Oxford: Oxford University Press, 2014).

3. Epictetus, *Discourses*, 2.5.15–20.

4. Epictetus, *The Encheiridion of Epictetus and Its Three Christian Adaptations*, 51.2, trans. Gerard Boter (Leiden: Brill, 1999).

5. Epictetus, *Encheiridion*, 17.

6. Epictetus, *Discourses*, 1.24.20; see also 1.25.7–21 and 2.16.37.

7. Epictetus, *Encheiridion*, 51.2; italics added. See also *Discourses*, 1.4.13–17, 1.18.21–3, 1.24.1–2, and 3.25.3.

8. *Heraclitus*, trans. Philip Wheelwright (Princeton, NJ: Princeton University Press, 1959).

9. Heraclitus—The Fragments, B70, website and translations by Ross Coburn, http://www.heraclitusfragments.com/files/e.html

10. Heraclitus—The Fragments, B52.

11. Mihai Spariosu, *Dionysus Reborn: Play and the Aesthetic Dimension in Modern Philosophical and Scientific Discourse* (Ithaca, NY: Cornell University Press, 1989), 15.

12. Spariosu, *Dionysus Reborn*, 15–16.

13. Viktor Frankl, *Man's Search for Meaning*, trans. Ilsa Lasch (Boston: Beacon Press, 1962).

14. Troy Camplin, *Evolutionary Aesthetics*, chapter 8, "The Game of Art and Literature," PhD dissertation, University of Texas, Dallas, 2008.

15. Pat Kane, "The Internet as Playground and Factory (2): Beyond the 'Play-Labour Nexus,'" *The Play Ethic* blog, June 16, 2009, http://www.theplayethic.com/2009/06/digitallabour2.html

16. Kane, "The Internet as Playground."

17. R. Zander and B. Zander, *The Art of Possibility* (Boston: Harvard Business School Press, 2000).

18. Spariosu, *Dionysus Reborn.*

19. Richard Rohr, "Grieving as a Sacred Space," blog post, January 3, 2003, http://www.jmm.org.au/articles/1266.htm.

20. G. K. Chesterton, "On Running after One's Hat," in *All Things Considered* (New York: J. Lane, 1908).

21. Karl Popper, *The World of Parmenides: Essays on the Presocratic Enlightenment*, ed. Arne Peterson (New York: Routledge, 1998).

22. From Nietzsche's *Thus Spoke Zarathustra*, in *The Portable Nietzsche*, trans. Walter Kaufmann (New York: Penguin, 1954).

Chapter 3

Dark Play

The silver leaves of Mrs. Knight's maple slowly gave up their glimmer to the dusk of that Labor Day's evening. School would start the next day, so we celebrated our passing with one last game of hide-and-seek.

Rocky was undisputedly the Best Hider but secretly I considered myself the Best Seeker. Wanting to prove myself, I volunteered to be *It*, skirting the usual "one potato, two potato" selection process. Eyes covered, I counted to 100 against the maple's trunk while everyone scattered.

Within minutes, I knocked off the less concealed with rapid fire series of "one, two, three, I see you" I caught Wanda in Mr. Carter's window well and outran Billy to the tree. Now I only had to find Rocky. I knew catching him would be hard. Since July, he had bragged about his "perfect hiding place," which he vowed to use during the last game of the summer. It came down to him and me. The suckers, who had already been caught, tried to outshout one another with bets up to a "kazillion dollars" on whether I would find Rocky.

Every strategy was used to spot him. I spiraled out from home, methodically searching improbable hiding places, while keeping a foot and eye toward the silver tree. I explored locations that no one had used that summer, but no Rocky. When I picked Rocky's baseball cap off Mrs. Fleiger's evergreens, I thought I was getting warm, and when I spotted his tee-shirt draped over Mr. Gunther's backyard fence, I knew I was getting hot. Then I inspected my own favorite hiding place. There, on top of Mrs. Knight's garage roof I discovered Rocky's red bandana. Hope boiled into rage when I realized he had bamboozled me.

I threw Rocky's belongings against the tree while his fans heckled me. "He's a freak, he can't seek!" They urged my surrender, but I refused to concede. Determined to locate Rocky, I scratched my brain for ideas and rubbed my rabbit's foot for luck.

Dusk shaded into dark, and soon parents were calling children for baths before their great migration back to school. When my last playmate skipped home, I gave up the ghost. I wailed out what I dreaded, "Olly olly oxen free!" and waited for Rocky to materialize.

As I stood under the tree, trying to catch the direction of his emergence, I felt a drip. I wiped what I thought was sap from my hair. Fingering a bubbly, gooey glob, I realized it wasn't sap; it was SPIT!

I looked up through limbs and darkness. There, high in the maple, sat a shirtless Cheshire cat. For a long moment I just looked at his impish smile with my mouth open. Rocky was home free.

"How'd ya do that?," I begged, trying to figure how he climbed the tree undetected.

"Guess!" he said defiantly.

When my mother whistled me home for the third time, I spit into my hand and slapped it on Rocky's bare back. Without flinching, he accepted this boyish payback, which somehow conveyed my congratulations as well.

THE DARK SIDE OF PLAY

Over time this childhood episode with Rocky has become an incident of joy and curiosity for me. It resurrects fond memories of the old neighborhood and the games of summer that preoccupied me and my playmates. I remember the fun of competition, the desire to be the best, and the pride of winning. But I also remember my boyhood dread of losing. My parents extolled the virtues of being a "good loser," but their counsel seemed shallow in the contentious waves of my neighborhood.

For us kids, games weren't about winning and losing; they were about *being a winner* or *being a loser*. We didn't simply compete for fun; we competed with our identities on the line. Who could run faster, think quicker, fight harder, or hide and seek better—these things established a pecking order. One day we'd be champions and the next freaks, depending on the outcome of the latest contest. We spit out our contempt and slapped back our retaliation. Like Humpty-Dumptys, our breakable egos teetered on an anxious edge between victory and defeat, pride and shame.

Fun is one of the hallmarks of play, and competition can certainly be fun. It stretches our abilities, teaches us discipline, motivates us to persist, and takes us deeper into the play than we would have gone. But nearly all of us can remember that childhood experience of being shown up—or cruelly showing up another—in the heat of competition. That moment when play turns nasty and becomes something else altogether.

The memory of Rocky's boyhood coup reminds me of the ways that play can morph into its many dark counterparts. They encompass the drive for supremacy that erupts from our reptilian brains and turns competitiveness into dominance. Likewise, fun can morph into frivolity, playing around into narcissism, and pleasure into decadence. This chapter examines some of these dark sides.

THE POWER PLAY OF DOMINANCE

Play rewards creativity, but it also rewards skill. Most parents want the best for their children and try to give their children every advantage. That might mean cheering their kid from the soccer field sidelines or haranguing their kid day and night about practicing piano. Success in these scenarios depends on perseverance and skill, and parents know that perseverance and skill matter. Soon winning becomes the sign of skill, and scoring that goal or perfecting that arpeggio means you're going to win at life too. Our culture fixates on success and rewards its business gurus and sports heroes with fame, wealth, and power.

Competitive play builds a child's physical and mental abilities. Ideally, it integrates mind and body while fostering self-esteem, confidence, self-reliance, and satisfaction. This play can promote fairness, assertiveness, courage, and a can-do attitude that pushes limits, rights wrongs, and lets us discover new and better ways to accomplish goals. It can encourage persistence, leadership, resolve, and meaningful contribution. The personal achievements of competitive play are earned and appropriately rewarded.

But when the rewards of competence and winning—praise, esteem, and even fear—become too important, when the competitive instinct becomes overused and unchecked, competitive play degrades into the play of dominance with its narcissism, manipulation, cheating, and cruelty. Winning becomes an obsession, and *play* is replaced with *game*. The need to maintain the privileges of domination trumps all other considerations. Self-esteem corrupts into self-absorption, self-reliance into self-service, self-confidence into self-aggrandizement, creativity into rules and control, and fun into relentless goal-seeking.

Toxic Masculinity

A gifted psychotherapist helped me understand how this dark side of play ritualized my struggles of growing up male. In a competitive culture, boys grow up in the anxious ambiguity between being a winner or a loser. A boy's social value is constantly scrutinized by peers who assume the culture's maxim, "You're only as good as your last game." For me, like so many boys, this meant constantly climbing a very slippery slope. My Catholic subculture raised the incline with its "be perfect as your Heavenly Father is perfect" expectation and greased it with its countless rules and regulations. We were constantly evaluating ourselves in terms of good and evil, success and failure, pride and shame, and winning and losing. At some point, winning became an irresistible focus in itself—because winning gave us power: the power to be respected, to avoid shame, and to be the one in the tree spitting rather than the one on the ground being spit on.

The play of dominance finds new and better ways to serve the imperialistic ego as it plunders, destroys, and annexes the good intentions of others. The dominating player cheats and views the honesty of others as stupidity. He crosses the lines of the social contract by using personal attacks to humiliate his opponents. He uses domineering displays of rage and in-your-face confrontation to shut down those who might object. Instead of assertiveness, the play of dominance uses intimidation. Instead of pushing the limits, it violates boundaries and rules of common decency. Instead of righting wrongs, it wrongs the rights and sensibilities of others.

Displays of domination are often associated with masculinity, and with good reason: the correlation between gender and violence is very high. There are endless debates about why this is, but we learn early that the real-life tasks for boys were to overcome fear with courage and to outrun the shame of being a loser—or at least hide this fear and shame successfully, with stiff-faced defiance, grandiose bravado, or stony silence. The commandments of growing up male in my generation were: Be tough; don't back down. Be a winner; don't lose. And, especially, be a man; don't cry (like a girl). A successful male identity was built on the central patriarchal virtue of dominance and the elimination of fear, shame, and sensitivity, despite the fact that this recipe for becoming a man meant one had to stop being fully human.

The Rules of Patriarchy

Boys in my neighborhood knew only one kind of play. Whether hitting baseballs in the summer or kicking footballs in the fall, our play was contest and combat. We were either heroes or goats. After spring rains, we pasted one another with mud balls and in winter we lobbed snowballs over erected forts. We toppled one another playing King of the Mountain, shot each other as cowboys and Indians, and punched one another, pretending to be Rocky Marciano. Backyard dirt piles were miniature battlefields, where we shelled one another's toy soldiers with plastic tanks and bombed twig fortresses with silvery toy saber jets.

We didn't play with girls, unless they wanted to play by our rules. Boys who played girl-games or with girls were sissies and "homos" who deserved contempt. A tomboy-type girl was occasionally included if she could prove her competitive mettle. Playing greed-oriented Monopoly and homophobic Old Maid with our sisters was acceptable on rainy days because they subtly provoked fear and shame and, consequently, intense competition. Our play was superior because boys were superior, as the pervasive patriarchy of our culture subtly conveyed to us.

Sometimes our boyish play deteriorated into cruelty. We slingshot squirrels and birds, pulled wings off flies, stoned water bugs dancing in streams, and smashed anything that crawled. We bullied other boys we considered weaker. Our neighborhood wasn't poverty-stricken; our mothers were homemakers and our sober fathers coached baseball. We ate dinner together and went to church on Sundays. We were good kids from good families, just having fun, like boys do. But why did we play so aggressively then? Why do we still?

The play of dominance connects boys and men through strife. Competition grounds mutual respect and caring and builds camaraderie among teammates and between foes. Men bond together because real and fantastical battles need to be fought. Opposition glues men together and gives their play focus and purpose. We stay connected because we have common dragons to slay. When men get together they play or watch competitive sports, work or discuss work, brag or complain about their wives and children, and ritualistically drink beer to free their feelings and salve their wounds.

This is connection of a type, but entirely too much credit is given to competitive play as catharsis and sublimation. One might argue, as did Freud (an undeniable patriarch), that the play of dominance releases and channels aggression into more productive and creative activities. While this may be true, the play of dominance—as with any play—ritualizes and integrates the pervasive themes of any culture. Play implants the tissue of social consciousness into the human heart. Our play reflects what we desire and value—or at least what we've been told to desire and value. As such, the play of dominance parades a patriarchal desire for power and control and displays and replays the values of safety and security from those who might control us.

Perhaps the trickle of testosterone was already having its militant effect on our bodies and zinging a few squirrels was only a spurt of preadolescent aggression. This bio-deterministic balloon bursts when I remember the girls in my neighborhood. They could be as vicious as alley cats. Besides playing dolls and house and jumping rope, they would scratch, kick, bite, and pull hair, while verbally flaying one another and daily betraying their allegiances as "best friends."

Maybe our play dramatized the storms of the mid-1950s. The East Germans and Hungarians had revolted, only to be crushed by their Russian occupiers. The communist Fidel Castro was instigating his revolution in Cuba, and Senator Joe McCarthy had recently assembled his paranoid cohort on the House Un-American Activities Committee (HUAC) to purge as many real and potential communists as possible. The Cold War between the United States and Russia was escalating, with both superpowers threatening to lob H-bombs at each another. General Mark Clark had announced he would blast the North Koreans with the A-bomb if they refused to honor the Panmunjom peace terms. Secretary of State John Foster Dulles termed the U.S. defensive policy "massive retaliation" and encouraged the production of nuclear weapons. People on our block talked about building bomb shelters, and one family did. Fear gripped the country, as it does today. Then it was communism; today it's terrorism. Perhaps stoning birds was an anxiety release. Perhaps by playing at being an annihilating force, we tried to overcome our own fear of obliteration.

While our Y chromosomes and those menacing events probably influenced our play, there is a fuller explanation. Long before the contentious 1950s, people, nations, and ideologies had clashed in the swells of patriarchy. While testosterone builds muscle mass and inclines us toward aggression, it does not necessarily override men's wisdom and compassion. Rather it is the tidal surge of *patriarchy* that ferries biology and ideology to their dominating extremes. In that current I only knew contest, cruelty, and the drive for power and control. Foes fought like old battleships slamming shells into one another until one sinks. In that current, the privileged have bigger guns and thicker armor. With superior advantage, they justify their intimidation and persecution of the weak as they plunder their resources.

This militant play of patriarchy presumes that all life is hierarchal. Scientific observation tells us that the stronger, the more clever and adaptable, and the faster-reproducing species survive and pass on their genes to future generations, thereby assuring their dominance. The privileged then consign this biological tendency to social reality. This is called "social Darwinism," which presumes that human social dominance follows from physical and evolutionary dominance. Because of privileges that came to them through no effort of their own—social position, family wealth, inborn intelligence, education, access to resources, or temperament—the advantaged come to believe that they are naturally superior and are entitled to the social, political, legal, and economic privileges they have been lucky enough to inherit. This belief in the rightness of their social dominance—which, among other things, dismisses evolution's overwhelming chanciness and humanity's creativity—allows the privileged to indulge in all sorts of abuse and neglect. Patriarchs assert that their intent is the survival, protection, and betterment of all, but their self-serving dissipations at the expense of others reveal the emptiness of this claim.

The Cultural DNA of Dominance

The play of dominance goes back far in our cultural DNA. It was a crucial part of ancient Greek culture. The Greeks viewed the game of life as struggle, strife, stress, conflict, and competition where the strong survive and thrive. Greek heroes took action for personal glory. Competition encompassed a masculine cultural stereotype, with an emphasis on strength, competence, aggression, shrewdness, and initiation. And in their religion and mythologies, Greek heroes were forever seeking the favor of capricious gods, whose favor was bestowed not on the basis of morality but of flattery, excellence, and devotion; the gods liked winners. It was likewise the ethos of Viking culture, expressed in epics like *Beowulf*. And it survives today in capitalistic culture, with its equation of success with virtue and the crude adaptation of "survival of the fittest." It endures in sayings like the one attributed to Malcolm Forbes: "He who dies with the most toys wins."

Nietzsche believed that much of human activity could be explained this way. Even such seemingly benign activities as the pursuit of truth were riddled with ego and dominance. He believed that we pursue truth, not for its own sake, but for status, a perversion of the will to power, which for him is the central motivating force of all life. A look at the history of science seems to confirm this. James Watson, codiscoverer of the structure of DNA, said that the structure was discovered largely out of competition with fellow scientists.

The 1960s focus on permissiveness and expressive freedom provoked a wave of interest in play and games and resulted in a new manifestation of this old impulse. In the 1950s, Gregory Bateson was already arousing clinical psychology's interest in play. Bateson and his colleagues at the Mental Research Institute (MRI) in Palo Alto, California, believed that human beings must play games because life itself is a rule-governed hierarchy of games. They believed that people play games with one another as part of everyday life and that these games dictate power differentials in relationships, which players manipulate to favor their self-interests. Clearly, this theory views play as control over others. Bateson and the MRI group influenced the burgeoning field of strategic family therapy, which is still influential today. Jay Haley of the MRI group and Thomas Szasz theorized that psychotherapy itself was a meta-game between patient and therapist. Haley thought that patients had to lose the therapeutic game in order to win back their emotional well-being. He regarded the Alcoholics Anonymous program as such a meta-game in which the alcoholic must paradoxically lose the game of control over alcohol in order to win sobriety.[1]

Psychologist Eric Berne, of transactional analysis fame, wrote a best seller called *Games People Play* that introduced a whole genre of books on sexual and manipulative game playing. Berne likened game playing to dishonest interactions between adults who seek psychological advantage over one another. He abhorred games of manipulation and counseled relationship honesty. Berne cataloged the top-dog/underdog tactics of attack and defense as abusive and passive-aggressive ploys that adults use to coerce one another. His list reminds one of the "prey play" of the "playboy" who "plays around," the PUA (pick-up artist) who "scores," and the golddigger's trading of sex for financial security. In this context, play becomes a manipulative game in which sex, security, and sensitivity are reduced to betting chips.[2] Even the academic study of play is susceptible: Brian Sutton-Smith in *The Ambiguity of Play* recounts how those who study play for a living fight for definitional dominance.[3]

Perhaps the best artistic representation of these approaches was Edward Albee's 1962 play *Who's Afraid of Virginia Woolf?* portrayed on the big screen in 1966 by Elizabeth Taylor and Richard Burton. This film dramatized the viciousness of interpersonal games and the meaninglessness of life without honesty. The lost child in the play could easily represent the phenomenon of play itself, abandoned to the games of life with all its manipulative ploys of power and control.

For many of these writers and thinkers, play had lost its joy. At best play had been been relegated to the service of seriousness and work; at worst it was exploited by our culture's predilection for power and control. They shone a spotlight on a growing cultural narcissism and its manipulative emphasis on power and control. Life continues to be a game, and "winning," as football coach Vince Lombardi once said, was "the only thing."

THE GAME OF RELIGION

Playing for power is a terrible distortion of the actual power of play, which is its ability to transform us and connect us. Nowhere is playing for power more sad and vicious than in the realm of religion. When it comes to defining God, the battle has no limits, leading to absurdly horrific wars. Enemies claim to have the right definition of God and, by association, his will and the specifics of his nature, desires, and plan. Tolerance, people, and, ironically, play and Spirit are the casualties of this deadly effort.

The problem with religion is that it is often a game, not play. *Games* connote roles, rules, purposeful goals, clearly demarcated boundaries, and winners and losers. Play does not. Play is an unpredictable and arbitrary flow, an uncertain and boundless process that has no clear outcome nor purpose. Games have outcomes, scores, and winners and losers, while play moves and unfolds willy-nilly continually, appearing as one thing and then another. Games have purpose, while play seems purposeless at times. Games suggest that the "gamer" seeks control of his or her part of the field or board. In play, the players open themselves to what cannot be controlled or predicted.

The game of control historically begins in reaction to violence, a breakdown in law and order, in the oppression of the weak and marginal. Society yearns for rules that will put a harness on our worst instincts. But, as we know, power corrupts, and soon the power that is meant to put a harness on evil evolves into the very beast that it sought to control. Religion as a game has control and concern for the outcome as its gods. That outcome may be as benign as hope for the afterlife and a dedication to good deeds or as twisted as submission to a totalitarian regimen of beliefs and behavior. As religion becomes more powerful, it is often defined more and more by a hierarchical structure, a complex canon of beliefs, ever-stricter rules of behavior, and claims of special knowledge—insider strategies, if you will, for winning the game.

It is true that religion has contributed to humankind with its thought, art, and organization, an expression of our best instincts to improve humankind's lot. But just as often, this game has undermined humanity through its religious wars, inquisitions, and rigidly authoritarian interpretations of the good, true, and beautiful. Religion is display, not play. It is an advertisement, a showy display for drawing people to its members. It flashes offers that one cannot refuse, like heavenly happiness and certainty about the meaning of life. Religion creatively displays through symbol and myth who God is and what he wants for us. It only asks us to believe, to suspend our questions and doubts, and throw our lot into its promises and power to get the deal of our lives.

What religion has failed to do is recognize the humble truth that it *is* a game. It has failed to acknowledge that what we call faith is, at best, a good hunch; probably more like a culturally biased speculation that lost its relevance long ago—and at worst a self-serving ploy to rein in the masses. Religion has taken itself way too seriously, failing to see that it essentially makes things up, that its thought is speculative and provisional. It intends to do the right thing but in its overriding sense of competitiveness has done precisely the opposite.

All of us have a hunch about Spirit. We call this hunch, belief, intuition, and knowing, and we call Spirit either God, Nature, Yahweh, Allah, Higher Power, The One, or The Force. When we play with our hunches, freely explore what might be, we are in a liberating playground. But when we move from speculation to certainty and zealotry, we leave the playground and enter the suffocating, rigid pews of control.

WILD PLAY: FRIVOLITY, NARCISSISM, OBSESSION, AND ADDICTION

If play is freedom, can there ever be too much? If we are most ourselves when we play, as Heraclitus said,[4] can we ever be too much ourselves? If we want work to be play and play to be work, how can there be a limit to its role in our lives?

Yet every day we see the ravages of play taken to extremes. Call it unruly play or wild play. It's the child who doesn't want to come inside after "Olly olly oxen free" to do his homework, the philanderer who doesn't want to quit the game after giving his vows, the alcoholic for whom the party goes on 24/7, and the players, the bad boys, the girls gone wild. It is the ceaseless recreation of shopaholics, computer game addicts, sports nuts, porn-seekers, and Facebook narcissists. When the freedom of play becomes an obsession to play, play erodes character and squanders potential.

Our culture's welfare seems to depend on the distinction between play as a *worldview* and play as a *lifestyle*. It can turn chaotically out of control when driven as a lifestyle. Play needs the steering wheel and brakes of social order. Although prized by romantics and rebels, play as a life choice does not attract the mature and responsible. While play may serve a full and meaningful life, it can also devolve into waste and absurdity. Wild play manifests as frivolity, narcissism, obsession, and addiction.

Frivolity

Wild play can derail even the most ardent of commitments. Activists in the 1960s rose up during unsettling days of protest against the Vietnam War, the military-industrial complex, and authority in general. But, determined not to be the letter writers and polite inquirers of their parents' generation, the young rebels brought a sense of play to their protests: the Summer of Love, daisies in gun barrels, Day-Glo VW buses, the Merry Pranksters, Woodstock, and "Be-Ins." While hippies substituted play *for* politics by "tuning in and dropping out," as Timothy Leary recommended, yippies tried to join play *and* politics. Such "play power" advocates as Abbie Hoffman and Jerry Rubin marched on the Pentagon, scattered play money on the steps of the New York Stock Exchange, nominated a pig for president at the 1968 Chicago Democratic Convention, and appeared at HUAC clad as Santa Claus and Paul Revere. Politics had never been so much fun.

But this "political play" movement ultimately failed because of its indulgence. The rebels would "blow weed in the grass" before, during, and after their revolutionary work. The hierarchal structure it needed to build outward was undermined by the anarchic slant of its foundation. It lacked sensible leadership, focused agendas, and reasonable goals. Indeed without plan, purpose, and discipline, it lacked everything that its targeted institutions possessed in abundance. Further, its moral integrity was compromised because some were more interested in play than politics and others extended play to violent ends in order to effect change. Play was displayed as a subversive tool without substance and suffocated in its narcissistic casing.

With their outlandish displays, perhaps the Merry Pranksters inadvertently stepped into a broader understanding of play. Hoffman, Rubin, Leary, Ken Kesey, and Norman Mailer may have unveiled how *all* politics is play, not just ultraliberal politics. Everyday play is a lighthearted, trivial activity. But play can also be a competition, a conflict, and, indeed, a political activity that involves power, strategy, and subversion. Even reactionary politicos try to subvert the dominant paradigm and create an alternate reality with their special uniforms, their banners and slogans. Perhaps it is a short hop from a team insignia to a fascist symbol, from the fun camaraderie of a baseball stadium to the mob mentality of a military parade or extremist political rally. Play can be degraded to self-indulgence but also turbocharged to dominance.

Narcissism

Play that has been degraded through irresponsibility is not just the woman who binge-drinks or the guy who calls in sick so he can play videogames all day. It can also be the trust fund baby who buys and meddles with companies for fun, treating the livelihoods of others as game pieces to toy with for a time and then discard when a shiny new object catches his attention. Elizabeth Spiers, cofounder of Gawker and former editor in chief of the *New York Observer,* told of real estate scion Jared Kushner's stint as owner of the *Observer.* She inherited Kushner's old office and computer and was confused to turn on the recent model Mac only to find it was "inexplicably running Windows":

> I summoned our beleaguered IT guy to explain, and he informed me that it had belonged to Kushner, who liked the design of Apple products but preferred the Windows OS. "So he was basically using a $2,500 desktop as a monitor?" I asked. The IT guy shrugged. . . . Frankensteining two products you appreciate into one product [is] creative, in a way. On the other hand, why did the newspaper's owner need a $2,500 monitor? How was it anything but a vanity object?[5]

Kushner's time as owner was replete with moments of unserious toying. He didn't grasp that the amount of content in the newspaper was directly related to the number of writers employed. After gutting the newspaper of infrastructure and human resources, he abandoned it:

A few days after Trump won the election, Kushner folded the now attenuated print newspaper and subsequently announced that the *Observer*, in its digital incarnation, was for sale. He probably would refer to it as a "lean" operation. I would say in his zeal to trim the fat, he began eliminating muscle and hacked into a few bones. I realize also, in retrospect, that he may never have intended to grow it or improve it. It was for him, in essence, another vanity object—like the beautiful, expensive desktop computer he used as a monitor.[6]

Kushner's father-in-law Donald Trump seems to be a similar player. When Trump was asked why he started his reality show *The Apprentice*—when he clearly didn't need the money—he answered, "For fun." One suspects he may have run for the presidency for the same reason. His profligacy with Twitter, his laxity in tossing around "facts" and accusations, all have something vaguely playful about them. When asked if he would accept the results of the election if Hillary Clinton won, his breezy answer was "I will keep you in suspense."[7] He clearly loved keeping the press off-kilter and uncertain, being a kind of merry prankster himself but one without ethics or principles. The uncertainty and freedom of play, when married to privilege and disregard for others, can be its own kind of self-indulgence.

Trump encapsulates another trait of play: the appeal to instinct and feeling and the abandonment of rationality. Play is possibility, a realm of conjecture and what-ifs, a welcome relief from factual constraints and a healthy imagining of what could be. But what happens when playful speculation is performed as politics? Trump is quick to claim that contests are rigged against him (not just the presidential vote, as he claimed, but the Emmy vote when *The Apprentice* wasn't nominated). The pedantic reporters who pressed him for evidence were missing the point. The whole thing depended on whether he *felt* it was rigged against him.[8] If everyday play offers a way to cast off reason for a time and frolic in the realm of possibility and imagination, an excessive sense of play in politics can lead to a permanent sense of unreality, a complete tossing aside of the anchors of fact, consistency, and rationality.

Obsession and Addiction

Addiction calls up play in unexpected ways.[9] The addict, like the hero, challenges fate through an exertion of will that confronts the rules, the gods, and the inevitable destruction to come. Engaging with drugs and alcohol—indeed any of the myriad behaviors that are liable to addiction—can seem a bold and exhilarating act of defiance that hubristically challenges fate.

Drugs and alcohol may first figure as a self-assertive effort toward transcendence, a yearning for enlightenment, an altered state of consciousness, or even oblivion, but it is misplaced and misplayed. Their use is a fantastical and ultimately destructive effort. The yearning embedded in their excessive use is nearly universal but the problem is putting it into practice. We need challenges, tests, or ordeals in order to push ourselves and our understanding, to expand our consciousness, and to use the old hippie phrase. But these challenges can tilt either toward defiance and destruction or toward toleration and acceptance, acceptance of the now, just as it is, instead of what it should be, what we egoically desire it to be.

Addiction can equally be a dive into frivolity, which challenges the seriousness of anything. Frivolity can be embraced to poke holes in the dominant paradigm, exposing its falsity, making fun of its sobriety, and showing the hollowness of its rationality. It can feel subversive, but the joke is on the joker in the end.

When do we know when we are playing the game of life well versus being caught up in addictive flow? It's easy to see how one mistakes destruction for creativity and the dark for the light. Both seek transcendence through absorption. Both seek a kind of sacred, otherworldly experience of consciousness. Both intuit that letting go or release is intrinsic to the process. Both sense that the range of happiness indicates the territory of the transcendent. Both recognize the powerful ecstasy of being seized by something beyond our control, something greater than ourselves. Addictions are cravings for activities that, in moderation, are part of everyday life: relationships, substances, food, TV, the Internet, gambling, risk-taking, hobbies, and sports—all of the elements of life, but unbalanced and undisciplined.

Ultimately we have to pay attention to how the mind works—or doesn't work. If our play results in confusion, dullness, and the extension of craving, it is addiction—the realm of escape or avoidance. If play results in embracing tensions but relieving cravings, it is the realm of engagement—to see what is, sit within the discomfort, and not turn away, to be aware of an itch but not jump to scratch it (which is the heart of meditation, as we'll see in a later chapter). It is the contrast of escape versus engagement, dullness versus clarity, anxiety versus peace, temporary pleasure versus enduring joy, craving release versus allowing release, being out of touch with the body versus in touch with the body, and a filled-in emptiness versus an open clearing. Play brings a sense of freedom and fun. Is addiction really fun? Do obsession and compulsion bring freedom? Dark play may begin in these things, but rarely do they end there.

Play brings us some of our most treasured pleasures in life: the warm summer evening playing hide-and-seek, the high school football game when you and your teammates were in sync, the witty banter and mischievousness of that group of friends in your twenties, and the teasing and exploration and fun of new love. But, as we know, play is liminal: it exists right on the edge between control and chaos, rules and freedom. And when it tips into wild play, destruction ensues.

CONCLUSION

Dark play results when our playful instincts run wild and *winning* becomes more important than playing. It's when we must get the glory, the girl, the high, or the most toys. Frivolity can ruin our potential for serious change. Narcissism will waste the potential of others, and addiction enthralls us. Worst of all, domination makes others suffer so that we can feel the animalistic thrill of supremacy. If play allows us the illusion of danger from a position of actual safety, dark play deceives us with the illusion of safety from a place of deep actual danger.

So how to overcome our ego-driven excesses? How to engage in the kind of ego-transformation that all religion has at its heart? My friend Sam put the problem this way: "Like alcohol, the ego is a tar baby: the more we fight it, the more stuck we become. It is cunning, baffling, and powerful. If we try to kill our ego, it will take immediate steps to preside over its own funeral."

Sam convinced me that fighting the ego is a losing cause. But my father's guidance during a childhood crisis showed me another way.

NOTES

1. G. Bateson, "A Theory of Play and Fantasy," *Psychiatric Research Reports* 2 (1955): 40–51; J. Haley, *Strategies of Psychotherapy* (New York: Grune and Stratton, 1963); J. Haley, "Paradoxes in Play, Fantasy, and Psychotherapy," *Psychiatric Research Reports* 2 (1955): 52–58; T. Szasz, *The Myth of Mental Illness* (New York: Dell, 1967).

2. E. Berne, *Games People Play* (New York: Grove, 1964).

3. Brian Sutton-Smith, *The Ambiguity of Play* (Cambridge, MA: Harvard University Press, 1997).

4. "We are most nearly ourselves when we achieve the seriousness of the child at play"; attributed to Heraclitus.

5. Elizabeth Spiers, "I Worked for Jared Kushner; He's the Wrong Businessman to Reinvent Government," *Washington Post*, PostEverything, March 30, 2017, https://www.washingtonpost.com/posteverything/wp/2017/03/30/i-worked-with-jared-kushner-hes-the-wrong-businessman-to-reinvent-government/?tid=sm_fb&utm_term=.50241f38b6b9.

6. Spiers, "I Worked for Jared Kushner."

7. Patrick Healy and Jonathan Martinoct, "Donald Trump Won't Say If He'll Accept Result of Election," *New York Times*, October 19, 2016.

8. Healy and Martinoct, "Donald Trump Won't Say."

9. Sutton-Smith, *The Ambiguity of Play*, 212–213.

Chapter 4

Flanking Play

I wished my little brother had kept his mouth shut.

When he blabbed at the dinner table that Billy and I had poured gasoline on a black ant hill and then torched its inhabitants, I wanted to strangle him. My sister crinkled her face and stuck out her tongue in disgust. My mom disgraced me with her usual "I'm disappointed in you, Mark," and lectured me on how I should not play with matches, should not take gasoline without asking, should not be so cruel, and should not play with Billy, who, in her judgment, was a product of a "bad home." She usually punctuated her scolding with lightning bolts of theological voltage: "How would you like it if God set you on fire?" she flashed, simultaneously suggesting my analogous identity with both God and ants and my eternal damnation. My good mom tried hard to be sympathetic, but her Catholicism compelled her to forge her children's morality in a kiln of fiery brimstone.

I bowed my eyes and peeked at my father. He dabbed mustard on his bratwurst and forked a piece into his mouth. He then steered an appreciative smile toward my mother and said, "Good brats, Regina."

After dinner and dishes my father motioned me to the basement. I descended the stairs like a heretic about to face the inquisitor's rack, but he surprised me with, "Ever see an ant hotel?" He cleared the counter and said, "Go to the garage and get some 1x4 scrap lumber." I ran to the garage energized with relief. Thirty minutes later, the ant hotel was finished. He fitted pane glass into routed groves and drilled holes in the top and sides for ants and rain water to enter and exit. My dad pointed upstairs and said, "Get a teaspoon and the jar of honey and meet me in the backyard."

In our backyard, we examined a black ant mound near the decaying soft maple. He dug up some nearby earth and mixed it with sand in a blue coffee can. Packing a few inches of the mixture at the bottom of the hotel, he said, "Drip a few drops of honey on top, son." He layered the mixture and I dripped honey until the hotel was filled and readied for occupancy. I nailed on the top, buried the hotel in the hole, and covered it with dirt. Satisfied, my dad said, "Now we wait to see what happens!"

Five days later, we walked toward the experiment. My dad knelt near the ant hotel, while I reverently cleaned away the dirt and exposed the glass pane. With a flashlight I illuminated this shrine, a network of tunnels with black ants clambering everywhere. The next day, I visited the library, read about ants in the encyclopedia, and checked out two books. My honeyed summer overflowed with black ants.

FROM FIRE TO HONEY: ON (NOT) FIGHTING DOMINANCE

I often think of my dad's ant hotel when confronted with the all-too-frequent examples of the world's cruelties. Caught up in the current of play, I had dismissed the suffering of those ants in favor of executing my power, just because I had it. As I watched their little bodies stiffen and curl in my incineration, I briefly experienced the intoxicating rush of unleashing destructive power that washes away any sensitivity for life. Something as small as this incident has helped me understand the insanity of Hitler or bin Laden. Offering a drug-like rush of power, the storm of dominance has blown throughout our history, seizing boys and girls, men and women, who forget the play of sunshine. Little do we realize what we lose in the process.

My father showed me a way to escape the intoxicating allure of power. In redirecting my energy from destruction to construction, he showed me a way to turn away from *patriarchy* to a wholesome and rich *masculinity*. He brought me back from the cruelty of gaming into the pleasures of play: the fun that resides in accomplishment, the sense of comradeship with our teammates, the taking of personal responsibility, and the pleasures of competency. My father and I built something together. We hammered and sawed and created and then were rewarded with what goes along with it: exploration, learning, and wonder.

When my dad helped me build an ant hotel, he did more than just show me another way to play with ants. He showed me a way to resist dominance that was itself free of dominance. In dealing with my play of dominance, his inability was his strength. Rather than the fight-fire-with-fire lecturing of my mother, he simply turned his rudder into a different current. Rather than attacking or defending a position, he moved out of the current of patriarchal pissing matches altogether.

Like my mother, some people who are fighting for the good try to fight dominance with dominance. These are the ones often known as radicals. But fighting to overcome patriarchy is simply more fighting and more patriarchy, reflecting the eternal cycle of human struggle that bounces from one revolutionary ideology to another. The outcome of fighting patriarchy is "the more things change, the more they stay the same." Dominion over dominion is still dominion, however nobly intended at the start.

My father offered an alternative. When we built that ant hotel, he modeled the play of hospitality rather than hostility. He welcomed life and fed a deeper hunger for life. With scrap lumber, glass, and nails, he showed me how to construct connections and camaraderie into an entryway to abundant life. Instead of dominance, he displayed care; instead of the natural ladder, he showed the common ground; and instead of fire, he used honey.

My father's approach had repercussions far beyond our backyard. By declining to either fight or submit to the game of dominance, he opened my mind to new views. The earthworks of my ant friends dazzled me with their intricate complexity. Their scurrying about in their tunnels demonstrated a fascinating paradox of chaos married with order and purpose. It took time to appreciate them, to see why they did this or moved like that, and I slowly began to understand that their slight oscillations suggested a kind of primitive yet clear "ant-talk." They had a definite social order, but unlike humans, theirs seemed designed for the common good. When I learned that my little teachers were "communists" because of their communal life and service to the larger ant citizenry, I gained a lifelong appreciation for complexity and contradiction. I learned that understanding our brothers and sisters the world over takes time and attention, curiosity and good will. I learned that we need to open the doors of our mind to learn who others are and what they might need.

When I think on the world's needs and alternatives to dominance, I'm drawn time and again to the term "hospitality." When we allow ourselves to swim in the current of hospitality, patriarchal thinking is left behind. The meaning of concepts like authority and success changes. *Power* stops meaning being able to control others through rank, privilege, and resources. Instead of "power over," it means "power for"—becoming a concierge, in a way, who draws on resources and knowledge to empower others along their journey. *Authority* ceases to suggest the power to command obedience for lower-rung subordinates and to punish their disobedience. Instead it recalls its Latin root *augere*, which means "to cause to grow and increase."

Authority rooted in hospitality exercises its power by opening doors and giving others the opportunity to spread their wings, just as my dad let go of his authority to punish and instead created something new—which he then relinquished to me. He arranged the necessary structures and then stepped back to see what would happen; His abiding interest and care were hands-off both for me and the ants. His play was to build and then relinquish his creation to us and to play itself. With his creation I might have responded with indifference or destruction, instead I got caught up in the play of his honeyed curiosity. The author of the ant hotel had released his patriarchal authority while continuing his care and concern. The hotel had ceased being "his idea" and "his creation" and became "our idea" and "our creation" to play with as we wanted. If there is an almighty Author of creation, I like to imagine that my dad's actions and release incarnated this Author's hospitable and caring authority in the continual unfolding of the play of creation.

In this world of hospitality, *mastery* ceases to mean control or the titles or accolades of public recognition. Instead it comes to mean the skill that results from intense, sustained curiosity and practice. My dad was an inventor who never sought a patent. I cut our lawn with one of his inventions, an electric lawnmower made from a heavy-duty attic fan that self-wrapped the cord around its rotating cylinder mounted on a frame. He was absorbed in developing and making things work; once engaged in a project, for hours and days he seemed lost in reverie. My entrée into this world was to ask him how things were made and could be improved, and he could talk about these things endlessly. Relative to the lawnmower, he said that it needed a clutch that would draw the cord without jerking it and that he was stymied yet intrigued as to how to do this. Failure was never a dead end or embarrassment—an unwanted polarity opposed to success—but an opportunity to learn; he embodied a "growth mentality" long before the term became trendy. His enjoyment was unraveling mystery and, perhaps, my sharing his interest in this mystery. He played masterfully, less because of the satisfaction of completing his inventions and more because he lived in the enchantment of inventive play. He would blush and dismiss compliments when praised for his innovations, not out of false pride, but because he had already been blessed and rewarded in the process of play itself.

In the world of dominance, *difference* is nearly always oppositional.[1] Differences rank and order the rungs on the hierarchal ladder. Difference designates what is me and what is not me as well as my position in the pecking order. It is used to order and rank, to privilege and marginalize, to elevate and persecute. For instance, in my youthful play I defined myself as a Catholic boy: different, oppositional, and superior to Protestants, girls, sissies, and ants, which, according to my youthful contempt, were lumped at the bottom of biosocial ladder. To define myself similar to a Protestant or girl—or an ant!—was incomprehensible.

In the world of hospitality, however, *difference* is not a matter of higher and lower, or central or marginal. Rather, similarity and difference become indispensable dialectics whose tension gives vitality to each. In my boyhood world, ants were no longer inferior beings unworthy of my regard. They became "friends" and little teachers about life. When I repaired their mounds after a drenching rain and added tiny twigs, blades of grass, and sand for their constructions, they became my pets. Their lives fascinated me, their community intrigued me, and their travels to the decaying maple and back absorbed me. I was connected to them; we shared life and living together. When Wanda, a neighbor girl, drifted into my backyard, she asked questions about my ants and invited me to see her gerbils. Differences faded into likeness and liking, and Wanda became a friend too.

NON-DOMINANCE AT WORK: THE CASE OF THE PLAYFUL ACADEMIC

Occasionally in my practice, I witness this shift in playing. During a restructuring of a large university's college into new departments, department chairpersons waged war with one another for faculty resources, offices, and classroom space. Anyone familiar with academic life knows that these cutthroat, territorial battles can rival the worst of guerilla and trench warfare, often with the same emotional carnage. My client Mike was one of these chairpersons. When this bright and sensitive full professor came to see me, he was battle weary and ready for something different.

Mike had begun the reorganization of his department with an attitude of dominance and contest. He had aggressively advocated for his department's share of the resources, trying to land his department at the top of the college's hierarchy. His entire approach was a game of one-upmanship in which the most important, prestigious, and successful department should win the booty of the best offices and the most generous budget. The problem is that every department was trying to prove they were the most important and prestigious—and viciously attacking other departments as lesser. The stress of the game was wearing Mike down, especially since his department was full of young faculty, largely instructors and assistant professors, making the prestige of his department hard to defend.

Mike needed a new approach, and he found it by playing hospitably rather than trying to game the system. Rather than seeing his young staff as an obstacle, he saw the opportunities and strengths that they offered. They were still fresh with idealism and adaptability, unlike their jaded colleagues in other departments. They were comfortable with cell phones and laptops and were open to unusual teaching and office hours. Mike called the staff together, explained the restructuring problems, the limited department budget, and the college building's floor plan—and then asked his young faculty for their ideas.

The faculty came through. Mike was giddy with excitement as he spread out the floor plan in my office. His instructors had discovered a vacated space previously used as a university preschool, which no one had considered as departmental space. As he sketched in movable work tables, space dividers, secretary desks, classrooms, library, and file areas, he gushed about the large floor-to-ceiling windows that would beam light to this large open area. His faculty agreed and even favored holding day or evening office hours, teaching daylong classes on weekends, working flexibly at home or office with their laptops, and being available by email and cell phone for student, faculty, and administrative calls. The faculty also favored working in the open area, which encouraged collaboration and teamwork. As my client explained the plan, he would interject, "This is fun," "I could do this for another twenty years," and as he finished, "Maybe our location in a preschool let me play with this."

Their work produced a proposal to the dean that would end the department wars and also save space and money for the college. His desire had moved from commanding resources and annexing space to finding a better way to serve a greater good. Where he once saw opposition, he imagined opportunity. Mike turned the differences between departments from problems to possibilities and from limited options to an unforeseen creation. His play moved from apparent weakness to strength, from misfit to fit, from disconnection to affiliation, and from depression to exuberance.

The dean approved Mike's reorganization plan, but unfortunately it was squashed by the university administration, which allocated the space for another college's use. Instead of being disheartened over hearing this news, Mike arrived upbeat at my office. When he told his faculty about this disappointment, they said that although they would be squeezed into existing space, they nevertheless could carry through on the other innovations such as using cell phones and email, teaching on weekends, holding evening office hours, and working together, which arose from their prior planning. Mike talked about the esprit de corps engendered through the planning process. Mike even said that the university administration made a good choice—a rare admission in academia—by allocating the space to another deserving department, who would be using his faculty's ideas. Formerly, Mike would have been depressed because his goal was frustrated. Now, in the flow of hospitality, he was buoyed up by the realization of a very different and unforeseen outcome.

Mike had opened himself to the play process in a masterful way. He had turned over his problem-solving authority to his faculty and listened to their inventive solutions. He distributed his control and let them teach and lead him, as he encouraged their fresh ideas and eagerness. He took what was and flowed in the play of what could be. We agreed to recess therapy when Mike said, "I get it. This is how to play with life."

NON-DOMINANCE *NOT* AT WORK: THE CASE OF THE AGGRIEVED DIVORCÉE

For every scenario in which giving up control and aggression has worked out well, it's easy to think of scenarios in which an approach of dominance seems inevitable. Suppose Billy and I had installed a honeyed hotel in a termite hill whose little red inhabitants were munching on the wooden beams supporting my father's garage. My no-nonsense dad may have introduced me to the effective use of termite poison. What about much worse scenarios? Would not assassinating Hitler be preferred over taking life under this monster on life's terms, as the play of hospitality seems to suggest? What about self-defense, euthanasia, or justifiable war? Do we shrug with a hospitable yet impotent "live and let live" attitude that ironically leads to greater evil?

My work with Nancy suggests a possible answer to these questions. A divorced mother of two preadolescent boys, she sought help for depression related to her parenting and dealings with her ex-husband, Paul. Nancy, a pediatric nurse, identified herself as a Christian with Buddhist leanings who was deeply committed to nonaggressive and compassionate action. She reported that, a prominent dentist and alleged drug abuser, had left her for another woman and refused to cooperate with their postdivorce decree. Nancy said that Paul owed $17,000 in maintenance, berated her in front of their boys, skipped and altered visitation plans at the last minute, and verbally abused her during their telephone conversations. Her boys' defiant behavior and verbal abuse toward her nudged Nancy to seek therapy.

When asked what she had done to address these problems, Nancy said that she prayed for things to improve, meditated to calm herself, tried to talk with her boys, and discussed her case with her ineffective attorney, who seemed intimidated by Paul and his attorney. Nancy said that she, more than anyone, understood Paul. She said that she still loved him, hoped that in time he might see the light, and that they might reconcile. After I interviewed her sons and her friend Jane, I invited Paul to a consultation session, which he angrily refused; Nancy's account of her circumstances seemed accurate. Nancy also added that Paul had physically and verbally abused her during their marriage, as did her alcoholic father during her childhood. Nancy also had consulted with another therapist regarding these abuses and the postdivorce problems without significant change.

A seemingly compassionate therapist would empathize, support, and offer ideas and resources. However, as suggested by her prior therapy, this tactic only reinforced her victimization. Instead, I asked Nancy if she wanted to hear my understanding of why she was struggling—with the warning that my view might make her uncomfortable. With her consent, I gently told her that, far from being peaceful, she was being quite aggressive, and that aggression took the form of persecuting herself, her boys, and Paul. That by accepting meekly an unsustainable and injust treatment, she was actually betraying her commitment to compassionate action.

Initially, this comment shocked Nancy, but the ironic weight of its truth kept her in her seat. I affirmed her nonaggressive and compassionate intent, but explained that by allowing her sons to mistreat her, by allowing them to witness their father's abuse of her, and by not taking firm action against Paul, she was teaching her boys the acceptability of abusing women, who might eventually be their wives and daughters. I pointed out how this drama was similar to how her mother passively taught Nancy the acceptability of being abused by men by not standing up to Nancy's father and by failing to protect her.

At this point Nancy burst into tears of sadness and anger, reflecting the impact of this truth. As she dabbed away her tears, I asked her if she wanted to hear more. I told her that her behavior betrayed her commitment of compassion for herself and her boys and that her alleged love for Paul was false, because she was permitting destructive behavior that was eroding his soul. I added that her apparently compassionate behavior seemed hateful and revengeful because by permitting this abuse to continue, she indirectly enabled this mistreatment and perpetuated the very pain from which she sought relief. Finally, I said that she was wasting her otherwise compassionate energy on Paul; she should consider expending her energy on better causes and stop betraying her commitment to genuine compassionate action. Still crying, Nancy nodded.

With this, Nancy was ready to take action. She retained a tiger as her new attorney, who vigorously argued and won arrear payments and contempt charges against Paul. She purchased a handheld recorder and informed Paul that she was taping their conversations for the court record. She enlisted various friends to witness Paul's absence for scheduled visitations and she took firm action with her boys' behavior. She attended Al-Anon meetings, confronted and began healing the emotional schism with her mother and father, and volunteered as a hospice nurse.

Overcoming her pernicious passivity and victimization was extremely difficult, but Nancy chugged along slowly but surely. Nancy realized that often victims are unwitting co-persecutors, that the overuse of a strength (compassion and loyalty) can quickly become a weakness (hate and betrayal), that naive powerlessness invites evil, and that compassion for others begins with self-care. She experienced play's paradoxes and its concealment of one polarity in its contrary. Most of all, she steered that play toward more abundant life through a genuine, hospitable compassion.

Superficially, my intervention appeared confrontational and harsh. At a deeper level, it offered genuine hospitality. You don't coddle the guests if the hotel is burning, rather you tell them to stop what they are doing and get out. Five-star hotels retain crack security and safety services for their guests, as does hospitable play. Caring for someone who sincerely wants our help requires our honesty at times. Allowing someone to burn in their own deception is an act of violence; throwing cold water on them, an act of hospitable compassion.

By absolutizing seemingly compassionate behavior, Nancy unwittingly perpetuated and hardened the play of dominance. Her righteous underdog behavior camouflaged her anger, which spilled over as hurt, aggression, betrayal, and revenge. This absolutizing of a principle or virtue, while seemingly high-minded, is actually a key feature of dominance. The prevailing consciousness of dominance elevates this principle and erects a ladder with its behavioral rungs to be climbed toward moral rectitude. The ladder creates a hierarchy of righteousness that often perpetuates a culture of moral superiority and conceals its inherent self-deception.

The play of hospitality, in contrast, tosses out the ladder and encourages creative thought and the contemplation of action, both proposed and taken. It encourages attention to the inevitable contradictions within the realization of this abundant life—the polarities of good and evil, better or worse, and indifference and passionate caring. The way these polarities influence each other leads to an array of paradoxical experiences such as detached love, hopeful acceptance, and creative quietude. Indifference influences care and unfolds as detached love, while care influences indifference and evolves as hopeful acceptance, just as my dad released his hotel's fate to me as we waited to see what happened. Each release their dominance and evolve into something greater, more interesting, and more complex.

NON-DOMINANCE'S BEST MOVE: FLANKING

While my boyhood friends encouraged complicity in creating our little ant hell, and my mother demanded obedience to her admittedly more humane standards, my father did something unique: He turned my attention from the polarities of good and evil and toward something that was less good or evil and simply more *interesting*. My selfish urge to dominate told me to march ahead. My Catholic training told me to turn right around and go back. But there from the sidelines was my dad, engaging in what we might call a *flanking* maneuver.

The idea of flanking has an unexpectedly large presence in our lives, from spiritual practices to creativity not to mention war and strategy, where the idea of coming in to attack from a side angle while your opponent's forces are concentrated at the front has a long pedigree. Flanking has many of the characteristics of play that we've dwelt on: it's an in-between, neither traditional offense nor defense; it's unexpected; it rejects the polarities of front and back, advance and retreat.

Of course, in spiritual matters, flanking steps off the battleground altogether. It's relevant to nearly all of the most profound concerns that we struggle with today—not just right and wrong, as in my ant dilemma, but control and wildness, growth and "stuckness," and compulsion and freedom. This became clear to me when I first met Sam, a participant at a retreat I attended who became a good friend.

Sam's easy smile and soft serenity drew me to him that Saturday afternoon. It was near the end of the Vipassana meditation retreat and the room buzzed after the ten-day silence. After asking each other "how was it for you?" the conversation flowed into specifics. Sam said he was an alcoholic, an "old timer," sober for thirteen years, and an "old student," meditating daily for seven years. I wanted to hear his story, but he gracefully had me telling mine. That was Sam. His natural curiosity and skillful generosity had me talking about myself before I knew it. Thankfully, our relationship didn't end there. We visited and emailed one another innumerable times over the years.

We all have cravings that lead to our own and others' suffering. Some have extreme cravings—addictions—that take over their whole lives. Sam liked to play and the riskier the better, but he lost over and over again. Sam had struggled with drug and alcohol addiction, since he was fourteen, with the predictable results: health, financial, and legal problems; divorce and alienation from his children; and suicide attempts. Sam tried to combat his addictions with the equally predictable solutions: willpower, psychotherapy, medication, and twelve-step programs. He said that he had "chronic bruises" from falling off the wagon so often.

Many years ago, Sam took his first Goenka Vipassana course at the suggestion of his counselor. At that time, Sam attended regular AA meetings and was sober for a year, the longest period of sobriety of his life. Sam understood the austere demands of the course and committed to completing the course regardless of any discomfort. Sam described this first course as moving from "brutally tearful" to "boringly agitated" to "peacefully detached." Sam continued his AA meetings, meditated daily, and began to again write consistently in his on-again, off-again journal. When we met following a course at the Dhamma Pakasa Center, we shared how helpful Vipassana meditation had been for us, and he gave me permission to highlight his experiences with consideration for his anonymity.

Sam got me thinking about the meditation path we had both just delved into and also about my practice as a therapist. He said that he used to think about service as putting yourself aside and helping others. He noted that AA and most spiritual disciplines tend to emphasize this ego–other duality that seems to break down into what's good for the ego is bad and what's good for others is good. But for Sam, not only did this thinking create an unnecessary conflict, it was just bad psychology and ironically undermined the goal of enlightenment. His words stuck with me: "We can't beat the ego; it will always win. Why? Because the ego—however deluded—believes it protects and maintains our very survival. It will cleverly thwart any attempt to undermine its authority. Like alcohol, the ego is a tar baby: The more we fight it, the more stuck we become."

His years in AA had made Sam realize that when someone falls off the wagon, it doesn't help to either placate or blame the person. Exonerating his selfish behavior as an unfortunate disease or blaming his character as sinful or narcissistic is ineffective. Blame puts the ego on trial with the ego as judge, and exoneration dismisses personal responsibility. In either case the ego goes scot-free to create more havoc. Sam said, "The Buddha knew this about the ego. He tried to beat his ego into submission with harsh austerity. He suffered to overcome suffering, waged war on himself for his peace. He also indulged his ego with temporary pleasure that led to his inevitable suffering from its addictive cravings. None of this worked. The Buddha finally sidestepped this whole egoic drama. He offered a Middle Way through the briar patch of mortification and indulgence by offering what all of our egos deeply want: happiness."

The playfulness of Buddhism consists precisely in this: stepping out of the war zone entirely and making instead what John Dewey called a "flanking movement." This flanking movement takes us off the battlefield and onto the playground, allowing us a new freedom. In the next sections, we see how flanking play works in addiction and twelve-step programs.

FLANKING ADDICTION

Addiction has a surprising number of touchpoints with play. Drug or alcohol abuse involves testing boundaries, altering the user's consciousness, experimenting, exploring, often sharing a kind of camaraderie with other users.

While these constitute points of coincidence with play, it isn't long before addiction becomes the referee and free play is replaced with compulsion. Without choice or alternatives, drug or alcohol abuse becomes work, even slavery—an activity that soaks up all of the user's time, money, and volition just to survive.

One of the most popular approaches to treating addiction is the twelve-step program of Alcoholics Anonymous. The cornerstone of contemporary twelve-step philosophy comes in part from a surprising source: the American philosopher John Dewey, who lived from 1859 to 1952. Dewey was best known for his writings on education and pragmatism, but he was also a psychologist. He wrote several important works of psychology and was president of the American Psychological Association in 1899. In 1896 he published an influential article titled "The Reflex Arc Concept in Psychology," in which he argued against a simplistic stimulus-response model of the reflex arc. Along with William James and others, he founded the school of functional psychology, and in 1922 he wrote *Human Nature and Conduct: An Introduction to Social Psychology,* which examined, among other things, the power of habit.

Dewey had a revolutionary idea regarding habits—that they could not be changed by sheer force of will. Orrin R. Onken wrote about this in his lengthy article about Dewey's influence on Alcoholics Anonymous.[2] He noted that Dewey believed that

> one does not change habitual behavior directly, say by exercise of will, but by modifying conditions and by intelligently selecting the objects of our attention. He uses the example of a man with poor posture. The man is told to stand up straight, or maybe he simply decides that he will stand up straight in the future. Making an effort to do so, he manages to stand differently for a while, but having no experience of correct posture he is largely incapable of comfortably standing correctly even when he keeps his mind focused on doing so. Once his mind wanders, he returns to his old ways of standing. His habitual way of standing is an objective condition that prevents improvement of his posture. If the objective condition were a spinal deformity, everyone would understand the problem. However, when the condition is habit, there exists a tendency to blame his poor posture on insufficient desire or will. This belief that one can bring about a desired result by summoning up a powerful wish and a stiff dose of resolve, is in Dewey akin to a belief in magic. It ignores the objective conditions surrounding the behavior and looks to a supernatural power existing in the mind to achieve the result.[3]

The answer for Dewey was to take up a flanking movement. Rather than address the posture directly through force of will, the man with poor posture, says Onken, "must take up activities which promote correct standing without requiring him to think about his posture." To this I would add he must take up not only activities but circumstances, social contexts, and people who do the same. This is why meetings are so important to those in AA and why those who attend say they are alcoholics years after having their last drink: cravings don't die but activities and context can be changed.

In addressing addiction, you can't be free by staring it down but you can engage in misdirection. You can change your material conditions, your surroundings, and your focus. You can keep a list of all the reasons to be free of your addiction, all the benefits, and read it every day. Or you can start with meditation and schedule the thinking for later. You can notice how much of addictive behavior is a *habit*, not just a *craving*. You may smoke in the car at the end of every day rather than just when you have a craving.

In this case, AA's approach is not to employ willpower. The advice is instead misdirection: immediately stop focusing on the cigarette. Get a drink of water, wash your face and hands, and brush your teeth. Sit quietly with your eyes closed and focus on in-out breath. Focus on—become fascinated with—the craving experience itself, its sensations, the thoughts you have, and your beliefs about this. Let it be, let it dissolve, take eighteen seconds to breathe, think of someone else and contact them. One of AA's best insights is the importance of moving out and making contact with a helpful person—or with helpful, compassionate intention on your own part. Walk outside, breathe the air, smile at people, ask how others are doing, help someone out, and pick up a piece of trash. Giving money and service helps you move from the old habit of self-centeredness into a different flow or play, the joy of release.

A prominent compatriot of John Dewey was his fellow American philosopher William James. James was also a pragmatist, one who believed in judging any belief by its outcome, not its roots. And he believed that philosophy is "the habit of always seeing an alternative." He was fundamentally uneasy with closure, certainty, and dogmatic absolutes; for him there was always something new, arising, developing, and evolving that we can both create and be open to. A. H. Walles explored these aspects of James's philosophy in relation to AA and its founder, Bill Wilson.[4] Many of these echo the principles of play, like pluralism—being receptive to multiple tries and techniques instead of slavishly following a playbook; as Walles writes, "Both James and Bill Wilson, who wrote the *Big Book of AA,* believed in religious pluralism, that is, there were many paths to spiritual conversion." Like playing the game of "as if," what counts is usefulness, not dogma or right thinking.

Both James and Dewey saw no value in attributing blame to a person struggling with a craving like alcohol. Their philosophy is evident in addiction theory today. Proponents of twelve-step approaches see the controversy between the moralists (who blame the alcoholic for his or her behavior) and environmentalists (who inadvertently excuse the alcoholic's behavior) as part of the problem rather than facilitating a solution. They focus instead on how to best help the person with the craving. As Onken wrote, "The Big Book states it succinctly, 'At a certain point in the drinking of every alcoholic, he passes into a state where the most powerful desire to stop drinking is of absolutely no avail.'"[5] This is a direct hit on the power of rationalism. A simple step-by-step exercise of logic—"Drinking to excess is harmful; ergo, I will stop drinking to excess"—will do nothing. What Dewey recommends is even more akin to play: "In short, the man's true aim is to discover some course of action, having nothing to do with the habit of drink or standing erect, which will take him where he wants to go."[6]

FLANKING EGO THROUGH MEDITATION

Meditation is a radically peaceful type of play. Even in the everyday play of children we find flashes of competitiveness and ruthlessness. Entire cultures like the Greeks were built on the agonistic dynamics of archaic heroism, a kind of power play that spotlighted violence and triumph. If modern nations display a more tame, rule-governed, ordered dynamic, it is still often just "politics by other means."[7] And dark play has the romantic appeal of freedom and creativity, with ego at the steering wheel but no working brakes.

Meditation discards all of these practices of dark play and hearkens back to the healthiest kind of childhood play. It's like learning to jump off a diving board: a challenge, a risk in the context of relative safety, and a stretching and pushing through previous presumed limitations. This has no obvious purpose; it's done for itself, to see what will happen, how one transforms and experiences reality for having done it—like climbing Mt. Everest "because it's there." It entails learning a new skill, testing one's courage, and pushing the limits. The way that meditation may change us is a challenge that anyone can tackle, no matter how old or infirm. And yet transcending ego—the ultimate practice of meditation—is the most difficult challenge of anyone's life.

Meditation involves practice, a kind of training that, like sports, yields neurophysiological and psychosocial effects, both short term and long term. Training in sports helps establish neural patterns and structures in the brain, moves one from effort to effortlessness, from work to flow, and from thinking to responsiveness, as one develops skill and muscle memory; eventually the period of effort and work becomes shorter and shorter, until one easily slips into the flow of the play. In both athletic and meditative training these patterns are instilled. Over time and with a concerted practice, the meditative consciousness will become more and more a part of everyday life, from walking, talking, working, and even sleeping. Meditation then moves from an activity separate from everyday life to a consciousness embracing everyday life. One moves from being *determined* by the play of everyday life to being *detached* from the play of everyday life through observation/meditative consciousness to *being* the meditative consciousness in the play of everyday life.

Meditation helps recapture the effortlessness of play. As a child, play was play. As an adult, play became games. In meditation, play is again just play, but without the "childish things"—egos and humiliation and domination—that marred them.[8] As one Buddhist stated, "Thirty years ago, before I practiced Ch'an, I saw that mountains are mountains and rivers are rivers. However, after having achieved intimate knowledge and having gotten a way in, I saw that mountains are not mountains and rivers are not rivers. But now that I have found *rest* [meditative consciousness], as before I see mountains are mountains and rivers are rivers."[9]

This rest, this effortlessness, is one of the best parts of play. When children first meet, they don't ask one another what they do for a living or ask how they know the host or hostess at a party. They don't posture and size one another up or ask a common acquaintance who each other is or rely on their wives or husbands to introduce them to someone. Kids just meet and say, "You wanna play—[dolls, tag, baseball, or monkey bars]?" An old fallen log becomes a ship on an ocean voyage with captains, crews, faraway lands, and sea monsters. A ball bounces into any number of games. Play is random, spontaneous, and purposeless; it's what kids do when left to their own devices.

Adults adult-erize play. They set up structured games and organized play groups so kids can enrich their motor and social skills with an emphasis on limiting the risk of anyone getting scrapes on their knees or psyches. They hypothesize that kids need play to release excess energy, to trim excess neural pathways, to learn how to solve problems with others, and to exercise their bodies and minds. The utilitarian list is long for why play is valuable for kids. However, their lists are drawn up from the adult view, not from the kids, who could care less how play is supposedly ushering them into maturity. Meditation offers a way back to the effortlessness and purposelessness of child's play, but without the fear of humiliation or the lust for domination. Meditators become participant-observers instead of strivers.

Meditation also encourages a radical stoicism in terms of reality. We all know the saying "Play the ball where it lies"—it means to accept the given, release any "coulda, woulda, shoulda's," and embrace the challenges and opportunities as they present themselves. Like kids on the streets of Havana making do with an old ball and makeshift goal posts, in meditation we take what we are given—pains, fears, discomfort, happiness, noises, or whatever—and work with *that*.

Meditation shares with healthy play the maneuver of flanking, just like AA does. Meditation and addiction are startling counterparts to each other. Addiction is a game that is notoriously hard to quit because it is 100 percent about craving. Meditation is 100 percent about *disengaging* with craving. But how does it do that? What does it mean to say that meditation doesn't try to "beat" the ego? What does this actually look like?

I practice Vipassana meditation, a Buddhist practice that emphasizes mindful breathing and the awareness of impermanence. Through meditation, the meditator begins to understand how cravings—grasping and clinging to things that are in essence impermanent—create suffering and how letting go of the cravings of ego—the wants, the fears, the avoidance, and the desires—leads to the cessation of suffering. But no matter what type of meditation a person practices, certain elements are almost always part of the game: sitting, being quiet, and letting go of thoughts. Through these practices, the meditator arrives at a mental space that is often called a "clearing"—a kind of empty field of play, free of manipulation. It is like the play that a spectator watches during a game, but the play is not outside, on the field; it is within.

Arriving at the clearing allows an awareness of the present moment and its undeniable discomforts. The discomfort can come from thoughts: I'm so ready for a drink. What's in the fridge? When will my spouse be out of the house so I can get online? It can come from sensations: breathing, heart rate, palpitations, a "band" around one's head, slight pressures or tensions, and itching on my face, hands, and other parts of the body. Or it can come from emotions, urges, and behaviors: feelings of irritability, boredom, shame, moving the body to get more comfortable, watching the clock, and counting down the minutes.

In everyday life, awareness of discomfort usually leads to efforts to mitigate it. But meditation is different: Instead of relieving and escaping these discomforts, meditation allows for the deep acceptance of things just as they are, right now, without exception. This is the key to meditation: to observe and accept rather than react and manipulate. The play of phenomena is in a constant state of flux, forever changing, and impermanent, appearing as one thing then another, like bubbles in a stream. The meditator observes this flux of phenomena—including thoughts, feelings, images, and sensations—and the awareness of this moment-to-moment play becomes the center of focus. Discomfort is noted as discomfort, not as a prod to fidgeting or fixing. Desire is noted in passing, as an interesting phenomenon. And through becoming this kind of participant-observer, a player rather than a gamer, the meditator can withdraw from the field of striving and enter a different consciousness.

Buddhism is dedicated to separating oneself from desires, fears, and power, and the meditator knows that craving is clever and will always defeat the frontal attack of willpower. This was what the Buddha himself noticed. He tried the ascetic lifestyle of denying and disciplining the body's impulses but found that, like Brer Rabbit caught in the tar baby, the more you try to control things, the more stuck you become both in what you are trying to control and in control itself. And just as Brer Rabbit pleaded with the wily Brer Fox to "Do anything you want but please don't throw me into the briar patch," so meditation asks the opposite of what's expected. It asks that we give up control, ask to get thrown into a briar patch, where we were born and grew up, where we feel most at home. It serves as a backdoor, a playful means to sidestep, outwit, outfox, and leapfrog cravings, to circumvent the agon of willpower and move the focus from battle to observation. One simply observes the craving in its fundamental components, noticing sensations, thoughts, and feelings with calm equanimity. This watching or "witnessing" of the sensations is what meditators call *non-reactivity,* not a counteraction, as in the case of willpower.

Meditation takes us down the road of a *non-dual play* where the underlying presumption of reality, duality itself, is subverted. Meditation is not a game against a competitor; it is an adventure within, to an alternative consciousness, while remaining within the one we live with every day. This is not a withdrawal from the power play of the world, but rather a way of letting it pass by without infecting or disrupting the "clearing" that comes with meditation. It's a little like being in the zone during an intense athletic performance or being calm under fire in a physical or emotional battle. The presumptions of our everyday reality—especially about power and control, success, wealth, and the rewards that supposedly gives us meaning and happiness—fall around us.

While the ego can create havoc like an insane dictator, it nevertheless is vitally important. The ego is the site of memory, motivation, decision making, and self-esteem. The trick is not to *fight* the ego but to help it get what it—and everyone else—really wants: true happiness.

CONCLUSION

Addiction is a game that allows no winners. Its unlikely and opposite twin is meditation, a practice that steps out of the game entirely and disengages with even the concept of competition. It is a reality-based, this-world practice that permits an otherworldly experience of profound peace and incommensurable freedom.

One common criticism of AA is that the program never ends. The cure never arrives and participation in AA becomes a lifelong affair. But perhaps this is not a bad thing. Like meditation and play, like love and progress and spirituality, it becomes an eternal present—not a mountain to be conquered but a view to be enjoyed. This doesn't imply a passive quietism but rather a way to bring the non-dualistic play of the spirit into everyday life.

NOTES

1. I am indebted to James S. Hans (*The Fate of Desire* [Albany, NY: SUNY Press, 1990]) for his insight into how difference can be complementary, instead of oppositional.

2. Orrin R. Onken, "Practical Mysticism and the Promise of Sobriety: James, Dewey and Theology in Alcoholics Anonymous," http://www.loris.net/aapragf.html.

3. Onken, "Practical Mysticism and the Promise of Sobriety."

4. A. H. Walle, "William James' Legacy to Alcoholics Anonymous," *Journal of Addictive Diseases* 11, no. 3 (1992): 91–99.

5. Onken, "Practical Mysticism and the Promise of Sobriety."
6. Quoted in Onken, "Practical Mysticism and the Promise of Sobriety."
7. Carl von Clausewitz, the Prussian general and military theorist, famously wrote that "war is the continuation of politics by other means."
8. As St. Paul wrote, "When I was a child, I used to talk as a child, think as a child, reason as a child; when I became a man, I put aside childish things" (Corinthians 13:11).
9. This aphorism occurs in many variants in Ch'an and Zen literature but is first attributed to Master Qingyuan in the *Compendium of the Five Lamps* (Wudeng Huiyuan, 1252). Cited in U. App, *Master Yunmen: From the Record of the Ch'an Teacher: Gate of the Clouds* (New York: Kodansha International Press, 1994), 111–112.

Chapter 5

Bright Play

While both meditation and the twelve steps help us drop our guns in the fight against addiction and striving, they were never meant to be ends in themselves. Most religions and self-help programs, including Buddhism, have much the same goal: ego-transformation.

Ego-transformation is a term for all sorts of concepts—selflessness, altruism, ego-death—whose terminology may be religion-specific: selfless love (*agape*) in Christianity, enlightenment (*bodhi or satori*) in Buddhism, righteousness (*tzedakah*) in Judaism, altruism (*i'thar*) in Islam. And the world's religions are remarkably similar in how they describe a person whose ego has been transformed: *It is the person who serves others.* The Quran cites those who "give others preference over themselves even though they were themselves in need" (Quran 59:9). One of the hadiths states, "None of you truly believes until he loves for his brother what he loves for himself" (Saheeh Al-Bukhari). In Matthew 25 Jesus praises those who help others: "I was hungry, and you gave me food to eat. I was thirsty, and you gave me drink. I was a stranger, and you took me in . . . because you did it to one of the least of these my brothers, you did it to me" (Matthew 25:34–40). Likewise Matthew 7 has Jesus saying "I never knew you" to those who said the right words but didn't practice service. These verses highlight that true religion is not mastering doctrine but serving others; Karen Armstrong calls it compassion-based religion, in contrast to dogma-based religion.[1]

The practice of meditation, the theory of social development, and the program of the twelve steps are equally clear. Meditation brings the mind into equanimity, which allows meditators to live their everyday lives without the interference of cravings or fears. By putting aside ego, we are in a position to practice *service*—to reach out, practice emptying ourselves, and giving others the focus. When we try to secure the things we think we need—safety or self or pleasure—we enter into the field of power play, where our grasping hands wreak havoc. When we let go of those same things, we enter the field of hospitality play, where giving hands bring help and love to others.

Social development theories like those of Erik Erikson or George Vaillant also model the process of ego-transformation.[2] These theories envision healthy human maturation as starting with personal growth, then dedication to spouses and children, expanding outward to ethical or charitable behavior at large. Likewise the twelve steps lead the addict down a path that ends in service to others. In fact, AA provides an unexpected analogy to all paths to ego-transformation. The exaggerated craving of the recovering alcoholic is a wide lens to understand all of our cravings. We cannot set up an opposition of self to other, as if battering the ego does anything but further enmesh us in its machinations. Setting our sights on serving God too often leads to serving dogmas instead. Serving others is where the rubber meets the road. All philosophy, all theology, begins with ethics—how we treat others. Compassionate action is what we can all agree on. That's why the twelfth step in AA is not to live happily ever after but to help other addicts (often by serving as a sponsor).

All of this can sound rather dour, though, if the emphasis is just on duty. Cheerless obligations are not only no fun—they are, I suspect, not as helpful to our fellow humans. Perhaps that's why the greatest mystics and theologians have had a playful element to their practices and devotion. Play in spirituality invites us to build ant farms instead of just "not killing ants." It opens us up to creativity and solutions and balance—all the things that allow real transformation to occur.

HOW EGO-TRANSFORMATION CAN BE PLAY

It may help at this juncture to go back to what we discovered about play in the introduction. What makes play "play"? Four key features are participation, fun, imagination, and liminality (or in-betweenness). These aspects of play inform Frankl's radical ability to exercise his individual freedom (participation) in the face of terrible circumstances. They inform evolutionists' and theologians' view of the universe of God's playground (fun). And they inform our embrace of the "as if" of religion (imagination). Where dark play—such as addiction, narcissism, or dominance—threaten to distort or falsify the nature of play, flanking maneuvers use these aspects of play to combat them. In addition, practices such as AA or meditation engage with the in-betweenness of time, allowing the player to experience a kind of eternal present, where we lay down our arms and embrace uncertainty and impermanence "one day at a time."

By abandoning the head-on assault of ego and addiction and careening off in unexpected directions, we join Heraclitus, the "grave-merry" man, and Socrates, the "merry-serious" man, who find meaning in the in-between world where play thrives. And we discover how play can be both metaphor and path for spirituality and ego-transformation.

Participation

As noted in the introduction, "First, play is participation. It is something you do, not something you receive or observe. And we humans like to do things—we were made with creative impulses and are happiest when we are doing the things that come naturally to us." Note that "observation" can also be, in the context of meditation, a participatory activity. This is observation as an active undertaking, as opposed to, say, observing someone else meditating.

Participation—being personally active—is a key definer of play. You may enjoy a movie, but that is entertainment, not play (although you may later toss around ideas about the movie with your friends, which may indeed be play). That one must participate in one's spirituality might seem self-evident, but spiritual movements vacillate in their focus, emphasizing at times obedience, service, loyalty to creeds, personal transformation, or submission to authority. Every religion has moments of emphasis on participation, and these moments and movements provide a basis for bringing play into spirituality.

Fun

From the introduction again: "This leads us to our second definition: Play is fun. Play combines effort with reward, rewards that are fairly close to immediate. Some rewards can be the product of play, but—to be play—the activity must also be its own reward. We *want* to play. If we don't want to do it, it probably isn't play."

Fun may not be the first thing one thinks of in relation to religion or spirituality. But a quick look at history reveals how desperately we need to consider it as essential. When religion becomes overregulated, overly strict, obsessed with dogma and rules, obsessed with achievement and performance—a matter of competition and winning—it heads into a dark, dark place. It is here that we find the Inquisition, the violence of ISIS, the child molestation in fundamentalist cults like the FLDS, the children in somber uniforms with no toys, no interaction with the outside world, only the iron-tight authoritarianism of the cult leader.

Thinking back to the research of psychiatrist Stuart Brown, we are reminded of what he found when he interviewed convicted murderers after the University of Texas shooting by Charles Whitman. He found that "most of the killers, including Whitman, shared two things in common." One of these is unsurprising: "They were from abusive families." The second is more surprising: "They never played as kids."[3] Brown went on to confirm these conclusions through many years of clinical practice, leading him to eventually found the National Institute for Play.[4]

Play and fun can be weather vanes, pointing out our current spiritual health. Good Friday is a time of sorrow and repentance for Christians, but when more days than not feel like Good Friday, when the dominant tone of religious life is guilt and unworthiness, then a correction is in order. Historically, interest in spirited play pops up when the church becomes overly controlling. Play as mystical release seems to fizz up when religion becomes compressed by asceticism, dogmatism, moral retreat, and depression. It can help to remember the theologians and philosophers who have found fun to be central to their spiritual beliefs.

Imagination

"Third, play is imaginative. We are not reciting a doctrine or performing a ritual. We are not enacting a series of steps that can only have one outcome. There may be rules, but those rules are not deterministic, not instructions so much as parameters. Within true play, there will always be the new, the unexpected, and the indeterminate."

In Book 11 of his *Confessions,* St. Augustine mentioned being asked, "What was God doing before he made heaven and earth?" His answer: "Making Hell for those who pry into mysteries like that"—a bona fide good joke if ever there was one. (Concerned with possible fragmentation of the early church, Augustine wanted certainty. One of my Missouri-Synod Lutheran clients liked to affirm, "Gus said it, end of debate!") But despite its tone of playful humility, Augustine's joke did not exactly sanction playing with the big questions of theology. Contrast to this Plotinus, the great mystic from 150 years earlier, who wrote in *Enneads III* that all hunches about God should proceed in a spirit of play. Before him, Plato wrote that philosophical speculation was the highest form of play. All of these theologians knew that they were playing with texts and ideas, trying to solve great puzzles, making clever connections, and perhaps even making things up in creative and helpful ways. For them play was both a method of inquiry and the subject matter of that inquiry.

Imagination is one of the core aspects of play, distinguishing it from, for example, games with their set rules. In spirituality, imagination can allow us to hold our beliefs in an "as if" experience. It allows us to let go of the rules of fundamentalist religion and try on our views of God and reality—not in a spiritual smorgasbord of picking and poking at the offerings, but as a deep dive into what it means to believe what we believe. We can leave behind the prescriptive dogmas and absolute certainties and instead acknowledge that, since we are not omniscient, we will always be acting "as if" what we believe is true. One reason why Michel de Montaigne is considered the first modern writer is his fearlessness in proposing ideas about the world. Far from being terrified of overstepping his bounds like Augustine's cowed pupil, Montaigne felt free to speculate, to toss around ideas on everything from Christian martyrdom to the advisability of ignoring one's wife's affairs. Grounded securely in his own tradition, he felt safe admitting just how far his mind roamed: "I speak as an ignorant questioning man; for solutions I purely and simply abide by the common lawful beliefs. I am not teaching. I am relating."[5]

All myths operate as if they are true. Their meaning and significance come from a pretense, a fabrication, and a play on reality and are grounded in the observation that fiction can excavate truths that facts can hardly touch. Science looks for empirical facts and fundamentalism requires yielding to doctrine, but imagination may offer the means to a richer spirituality.

Liminality

A fourth aspect of play is its liminality, its "in-betweenness"—which is to say the condition of being in between defined states. As we saw in the introduction, this is where you are "set apart from the everyday or positioned between opposites or extremes. . . . Rules and flexibility. Danger and safety." Play allows us to embrace ambiguity and uncertainty, without fleeing the "terrible cloud of unknowing," as Richard Rohr put it, into fundamentalism or wildness or nihilism.[6] We are imagining but also acting. Creating rules then changing rules. Acting dangerously but being safe. Venturing forth to new ideas and experiences but always within sight of home.

There may be no greater expression of liminality in spirituality than mysticism. Mysticism is one of those practices that finds expression in almost all religions, one could even argue in nearly all human activities. Religiously, it is generally defined as the attempt to achieve unity with God or an Absolute, often through an ecstatic or altered state of consciousness and sometimes accompanied by a belief in esoteric insights and special cosmic knowledge. The method of mysticism is the direct apprehension of Spirit that bypasses rational thought, an intuition involving tacit knowledge, disciplined by practiced meditation and adept teachers. There are mystical practitioners of every religion—from the prayer-based mysticism of Saint Teresa of Avila to the substance-induced trance states of shamans to the Islamic mysticism of Sufi dance.

Mysticism is not as esoteric as it may first seem. It can even be seen in such events such as Burning Man, the annual countercultural festival in the American desert. As one attendee said, "If religion creates boundaries, mysticism and spirituality efface them. In the transcendence of ordinary distinctions, peak experiences such as those encouraged at Burning Man give a glimpse of the ultimate, the infinite. It may seem absurd to suggest that Burning Man is a mystical event. But then, if it's just a big party, why is there a temple in the middle of it?"[7]

Where to Find It

So how do these aspects of play unfold in the great religions' great work of ego-transformation? Participation, fun, imagination, and liminality have surprising roles in this oh-so-serious pursuit.

HINDUISM

Classical Hinduism

There are many religions that embrace a form of play into their spiritual practice, but none so much as Hinduism. Hinduism has the honor of being the oldest continuing religion in the world. It started developing about 2500 BCE and has never stopped evolving. It has no founder. Hindus can be monotheistic, polytheistic, or atheistic. There is no definitive religious structure and no single, binding holy scripture (though many sacred texts). As Kim Knott writes, Hinduism "defies our desire to define and categorize it."[8]

It is a tenet of Hinduism that the world was created through a process of divine play known as *lila*.[9] The centrality of play in the Hindu creation of the universe is seemingly unique in world religions. Play is the classical feature of the divine in Hinduism, although not so in either earlier primitive religions or the later high, monotheistic religions like Christianity, Judaism, and Islam (with only a few exceptions).[10] The Judaic and Christian creation account is more *plan* than play. The all-mighty Creator actively wills creation and executes it in an orderly fashion. He then rests (plays in His leisure) only after the work is done—much like my grandfather did.

In the Hindu view, the Creator offers not a plan but possibility. Creation is the process of releasing possibility into the world and allowing us, as cocreators, to play with the toys the Creator has provided and to know the Creator through our participation in creation's eternal becoming. Through this participation, we recognize the absolute reality of suffering and pain and open ourselves to compassion and, in doing so, make the play of creation a little better as it goes on and on. In this view, the deity is not a tyrant or controlling puppeteer but more like a commissioner of baseball, setting certain physical rules and boundaries and then watching the games of creation unfold with minimal interference.

In the *Rig Veda*, the earliest literature related to Hindu thought, how creation came into being is clearly unknown. The sage-author of the Veda merely speculates that creation was a result of the One's breathing breathlessly or by its heat warming water, or a kind of inherent desire to create that began with light piercing the darkness. The author Ram Shanker Misra explains why creation must be the expression of play on the part of Brahman—the ultimate reality or divine process of creation:

> Brahman is full of all perfections. And to say that Brahman has some purpose in creating the world will mean that it wants to attain through the process of creation something which it has not. And that is impossible. Hence, there can be no purpose of Brahman in creating the world. The world is a mere spontaneous creation of Brahman. It is a *Lila*, or sport, of Brahman. It is created out of Bliss, by Bliss and for Bliss.[11]

This aspect of Hinduism is key because it is distinct from the "volitional" creation of most other religions. As Misra writes, "Lila indicates a spontaneous sportive activity of Brahman as distinguished from a self-conscious volitional effort. The concept of Lila signifies freedom as distinguished from necessity."[12] Sri Aurobindo, the renowned twentieth-century Hindu mystic, had a similar insight. In his book *The Life Divine*, Aurobindo intuited that play was not only the constant creation and re-creation of worlds but the Creator's self-creation and identity. He writes that the Creator creates and re-creates "Himself in Himself for the sheer bliss of that self-creation, of that self-representation—Himself the play, Himself the player, Himself the playground."[13]

Hinduism thus offers the very first illumination of how play can be a vehicle for ego-transformation. Lila is the concept of play for joy and delight rather than winning or gain. It is expressed in the legend of the *gopi*, female cowherds who come to dance with Krishna when he calls.[14] It is a sacred process of leading humans to God. Krishna dances and plays his alluring *maya* or earthly form to his devotees who are seized by this resplendent beauty. Then Krishna disappears, and in his absence, the cowherd women wait and watch for his return, creating a hide-and-seek play that deepens the devotees' realization and appreciation of God.[15] This play totally absorbs the devotee. God's magnificence draws us to him; his evaporation both withdraws and deepens our soul's relationship to him.

This process is actually very common in everyday life. We are attracted to someone or something—often overwhelmingly. Soon the initial infatuation fades, but if we are lucky, love moves from excitement to commitment to devotion. What makes our lives meaningful is commitment, the courageous playing through difficulty, a devotion to a partner and an unknown future. As long as we only look for the intoxicating music and the dance of passion, we will never deepen our play. It is in between the states of engagement and endurance, reminiscent of the gopis' relationship to Krishna—now here, now away, now playing, and now waiting—that we develop the kind of devotion that transforms the ego.

Hinduism, with its emphasis on freedom, provides multitudes of stories and many paths to liberation, avoiding the judgmental pitfalls of dogma or orthodoxy. The trickster god Krishna employs the deception that reveals, the trick that teaches, and the illusion that enlightens. In illusive role-playing, he shows how to "take on" identities, how to enter and embrace the play of "as if," identifying with the deity as a path to enlightenment. By releasing ourselves to the process of play, becoming absorbed in play, we can leave behind the usual understandings of worldly reality and shed the illusions that surround it. Scholar William Sax notes that *lila* refers, secondarily, to a type of religious drama performed in India, in which actors adopt the identities of gods;[16] for actors and audiences alike, this is another way that "playing" can be a transformative religious experience.

The Goddess Kali

She was wild and unpredictable. She was a screamer who laughed at the funny and cruel. She'd create elaborate games, pull wings off of insects and birds alike, and play lovingly with little children. She also would whack the neighborhood bully and friends alike with her tennis racket, sometimes just because she felt like it. We called her "Crazy Judy."

Judy was my older sister's obsession, and she was constantly hurt by Judy's excesses and on-again–off-again friendship. Her tears and smiles clued us in on the kind of day she had had with Judy. Regardless, she would always return to the perpetual excitement Judy offered. Judy's feisty ambiguity both intrigued and scared me. One day Judy was screaming obscenities and threatening my sister with her tennis racket. I grabbed the racket and told Judy to stop. She flared and began kicking me and biting my arm. I tried to retreat with the buzzing of "no hitting girls" in my head. Soon I was on the ground, covering my head, as she whacked and kicked and shrieked like a maniac. Thankfully her mother stopped the onslaught. My body healed, but to this day I have a twinge of panic whenever I meet a woman named Judy.

Near Calcutta in northeastern India, there roams a goddess worse than Judy. She is the unfathomable, all-powerful, and dark goddess Kali. Considered a manifestation of Shakti, the feminine energy of the universe, the Bengali Saktas worship Kali. She is a terrifying and capricious goddess who births then devours her child. Like Shiva, Shakti's consort, she creates and destroys worlds like a wanton child who repeatedly fashions and kicks down sand castles. This *devi* is a magician who masks and reveals herself with her illusionary *maya*, a naked seductress manipulating the desires of men with her sexual power, a warrior who laughs when she severs heads and wears them as a garland, and also the mother on whose belly rain falls and life sprouts.

No discussion of Hindu conceptions of play would be complete without a mention of Kali. Her antics are her endless and incomprehensible *lila*, her divine play. She is the black tongue of Agni, the fiery goddess of the *Rig Veda*. She is the fearsome emanation from Durga's brow in the *Puranas*. The eighteenth-century poet-mystic Ramprasad Sen wrote devotional songs about Kali's play—still loved, recorded, and sung by her followers today. Ramprasad describes Kali and her *lila* as mad (insane and out of control), frightful (heartless, cruel, unpredictable, and untrustworthy), and deceptive (gamy, disguised, deluding, and subversive). Not exactly Mother Teresa!

Unlike the Greek and Roman deities, Kali is not swayed by heroism and hubris, gifts and gratitude. No human action can persuade her to intercede and give favors or remove suffering. Her play is totally free, unbounded by the world and its needs. Consequently, rituals, songs, and ceremonies to her seek nothing from her. They merely recognize and honor, often lavishly, her power and presence. Her followers complain and rage, like Job, at their goddess, but this in no way cancels their devotion to her.

Why would anyone be drawn to, much less worship, this apparent agent of evil? History suggests that Kali worship was a reaction to the Brahman (Advaita Vedanta) ideal of pure, non-dual enlightenment that entailed fleeing the material world and its illusions. Unlike these world-denying ascetics, Kali devotees affirmed life as hard-core real and reality itself as intrinsically dual. Human and divine, matter and spirit, body and soul, good and evil, birth and death, pleasure and pain, and cruelty and compassion are taken as the interacting and necessary sides of the same coin. Kali encompasses the whole coin and her worship embraces the entire spectrum of life and its dualities just as they are. Like life itself, Kali is ambiguous, arbitrary, and uncertain. Her tantric devotees face the devi's curse of death head on, opening themselves to all that life has to offer, both good and bad. They courageously embrace doubt, fate, and absurdity. They live for today, and find meaning in what is, rather than what is wished for.

This perspective goes to the heart of her play. Her *lila* is infinite, endless, risky. It is without rules, has no particular goal, and is random and unpredictable. She rewards and kills demons and innocents alike. Life itself is the full participation in Kali's *lila*; its meaning: total liberating freedom.

The example of Kali's dark play may seem an unlikely path to ego-transformation, but her radical sense of freedom has inspired followers both ghastly and admirable. Before the British crushed their activities in 1830, a fraternity of Kali devotees called the Thuggees (the source of the English word "thug") robbed and strangled travelers in India. Considered the world's first "mafia," they killed over two million people between the thirteenth and nineteenth centuries. They believed that each robbery and subsequent murder delayed by 1,000 years the arrival of the Kali age, when all would be destroyed.

Orthodox Hindus generally reject the misguided violence and sexual excesses of this "left-handed" tantric tradition as dangerous and inconsistent with the emphasis on compassionate wisdom and genuine liberation seen in the Hindu scriptures. They also caution that the mythical antics of the gods are not models for human activity. A brighter form of Kali devotion might be seen in her follower Ramakrishna, a nineteenth-century yogi whose followers founded a mystic order and monasteries after his death. Ramakrishna is known for his embrace of diverse traditions and assertion that all religions are true. He famously became a Muslim for three days, then later a Christian for three days. Ramakrishna "put on" belief, play-acting "as if" each religion were true—and finding such play-acting a fully authentic route to ego-transformation. All spiritual practices had the goal of God-realization, and all practices had the capacity to achieve that goal.

Modern Western Yoga

While Hinduism is the oldest religion in the world, its most recent incarnation in the West has taken the form of yoga—the practice of meditation, stretching, and more that exists within the non-Hindu cultures of the West. In a practice that is sometimes approached with deadly seriousness, some modern yoga teachers are proponents of bringing the spirit of play into yoga, like Sadie Nardini, director of yoga at East West Yoga in Manhattan. She "calls herself 'reverently irreverent,' and said she runs a kind of 'punk rock' practice. . . . 'People are moving away from what I call the Madame Tussaud's yogi, frozen in a super-serious face, and instead want to rediscover the joy of living, even on the mat.'"[17] Nardini explains: "People laugh at first and then get teary chanting Bon Jovi," she said.

While these adjustments in your local yoga class may seem a far cry from the complex play of *lila* theater or Ramakrishna's putting-on of other religions, there are yogic benefits to this small shift: "'When you laugh, you open your heart to reality,' she said. 'Truth is there, deep in that laughing place.'"[18] Yoga instructor Havi Brooks presents a rubber duck in class as her co-teacher. Her perspective is this: "Does it make me better at yoga if I take myself really seriously? No."[19] Instructor Karen Cohen puts it this way: "The ability to cultivate joy and lightness in our lives is one of the principal aims of true yoga: the bringing of opposing qualities into a productive harmony. . . . Joy is healthy. A bit of goofy is good. Seeing and experiencing the humor in tough situations—that is yoga. Yoga teaches us to enjoy and embrace paradox."[20]

Or as Kelly McGonigal, onetime editor in chief of the *International Journal of Yoga Therapy*, says: "Ego is the enemy of both humor and yoga."[21]

A Detached God and a Playing Human

Being God's playful accident frees us yet places responsibility for the world squarely in our hands. Luxuriating in a planless and purposeless reality for its own sake, the Hindu view of God disavows any rigid plan for our lives or our world. It removes the insanity of fundamentalists found in all religions who insist they know God's plan and will and have a divine mandate to impose it.

God's distance also invites great responsibility. Mature spirituality means recognizing that God is not implementing a program and that we have utter responsibility for the planet and what happens in it. Play entails a profound responsibility for our own outcomes. With freedom and choices, we make the world what it is. We still have to climb and negotiate life's cliffs and crevasses. This is a matter of initiative, purpose, and, especially, responsibility. While we may realize the effortless and blissful play of the Trinity, we still have to cook dinner and take out the garbage. This is the created world, and this world is our responsibility. The creation of the world might be an unintended accident of God's play, but it is ours to fix up and make better.

This ground of play frees us to live a hearty spiritual life. Our birthright gives us the opportunity to play the spirited play that flows everywhere and saturates our being. It lets us delight in the play that plays its own play eternally before time and creation just as it is, just for the divine fun of it. The Hindu view of spirituality as play makes life become more of an adventure than a forced march, more of a discovery than a sure plan, and more a full present of possibilities than a preordained future of scripted outcomes.

JUDAISM

While the Jewish Bible has its fair share of rules and military exploits, hidden among the *begat*s and the walls tumbling down are nods to a playful approach to God.

Hasidism and the Besht

Judaism is believed to have been founded by Abraham in roughly 1800 BCE. As in any religion, there have been multiple movements and sects along the way, one of which is Hasidism. The founder of Hasidic Judaism was Israel ben Eliezer (c. 1700–1760), also known as the Baal Shem Tov or the Besht. The Besht was a Jewish mystical rabbi who emphasized the principle of *devekut*—communion, or always having God in mind. He opposed the cordoning off of God or spirituality within purely religious acts or arenas and instead urged people to maintain a continuous communion with God in the midst of their daily routine and their interactions with others. He expressed the beauty of this integration, saying that when a "man is occupied with material needs, and his thought cleaves to God, he will be blessed."[22]

His view was of God playing joyfully in and through the universe, allowing the Besht to view life and what happens in life as extremely optimistic regardless of how bad things were. For the Besht, God—the source of all that is good and immanent in the world—allows us to understand that there is something good in all, even sin and suffering. The Besht viewed humans as intrinsically good, although blind or unenlightened. Sin was a result of stupidity and needed to be explained, not condemned. The Besht believed that no one is so low that they cannot raise him- or herself to God. He believed the sacred was in scum—much like the Tao, which is said to sink to the lowest level.

The Besht also emphasized that asceticism or renunciation is *not* pleasing to God. Denial of life is a denial of God and God's expression as ecstatic joy. Like most Jewish traditions, the Besht emphasized life in this world, not denial or turning away from life in hope of a better life in the hereafter. The Besht did not like the ascetic versions of the Kabbalah that disdained the world. The world of matter was God's creation and manifestation and needed to be loved as part of all life. He also stressed that care for the body was equal to and inseparable from care of the soul. He opposed fasting or any other type of withdrawal from daily life.

The Besht also found the strict and sanctimonious Talmudic view inappropriate, too often emphasizing the law over the growth of the inner life of the human heart. In this he joins reformers from all religions who, with a certain regularity, attempt to get believers to shed the carapace of rituals and rules and adopt a focus that instead brings them into communion with God and into a heart-attitude of kindness for others. In just such a way the Taoist Chuang-Tzu bemoaned the laborious forms and rules of Confucianism, and Erasmus of Rotterdam tried to get Catholics and Protestants alike to become less interested in sacraments and doctrine and more interested in not killing each other. Like these reformers eager to highlight the heart over the outward forms of religion, for the Besht spiritual progress was less a matter of intellectual study and formal ritual than of the gradual realization or intuition of humanity's direct relationship with the Creator and life as his creation. Prayer, to the Besht, was a joyful release to God, not a petition seeking God's favor. Bliss and gratitude to God were primary in the Besht's prayer.

The Besht was skeptical of the praying and weeping of sinners practiced by Isaac Luria (1534–1572), the founder of modern Kabbalah, because focusing on guilt and worthlessness was incompatible with the Creator's intention for joy in connection with him. Fear of God should be only the first step, followed by love, release, or surrender to God who is joyfully playing (creating and re-creating) in the world. What is compatible is embracing God's joy fully in ecstatic celebration.

This deep and joyful union with God is both means and end of all life and authentic religion that occurs in this world, not in another. Consider this story: In Constantinople, where the Besht stopped on his intended journey to the Land of Israel, he was received with unusual hospitality by a worthy couple who were childless. In return for their kindness Besht, when departing, promised them that they should be blessed with a son and rendered this possible by the utterance of the Sacred Name. Now, to do this was a great sin, and scarcely had the words of the incantation passed Besht's lips when he heard a voice in heaven declaring that he had forfeited thereby his share in HaOlam HaBa (the world to come). Instead of feeling unhappy over such a fate, Besht called out joyfully: "Blessed art Thou, O Lord, for Thy mercy! Now indeed can I serve Thee out of pure love, since I may not expect reward in the future world!" This proof of his true love for God won pardon for his sin, though at the expense of severe punishment. Like the bodhisattva who vows to return to the grind of samsara until all sentient beings are enlightened, the Judaic lover of God should serve in this world rather than focusing on leisure in the next.

The devout Hasidic Jew understands that the world remains in darkness awaiting the evolved and radiant glory of a future Messiah. Another Jewish tradition likens human souls to fading embers in a cold hearth ready to spark to flames on the arrival of the Messiah. This return and this relighting are aided by the work of *tikkun olam*, "repairing the world" by gathering together the sparks of goodness and unifying them through acts of goodness, from rejecting idolatry to prayer to service to society. Through giving of themselves to others, such people bring the good sparks together, preparing the kingdom, infusing the holy into the mundane through every act in every moment of their lives.

However, for the Hasidic mystic (*tzadik*), there's an additional aspect to the return of the Messiah. These mystics don't deny that the Messiah's arrival will be a future, physical event. Yet, in their mystical experience, they simultaneously realize that the Messiah has already secretly arrived and has begun his healing and sanctifying mission through them. They understand that the Messiah is concealed (playing hide-and-seek) from those whose consciousness remains only in a rational, space-time dimension. This circuitous journey is intrinsically humorous: We leave home on a quest for the divine, only to return and find the divine that has always dwelled within the home we left, in the human heart. This humor is not a balm for anguish or a tickle to seriousness; it is the disposition of the enlightened person who laughs at his own silliness of presuming that reality is "out there."

This Hasidic notion of an always-already Spirit also suggests that an afterlife or heaven is superfluous. The afterlife in Christian and Muslim traditions offers an explanation that compensates for the injustice of this life; but in the process they create a different set of problems that plague humanity, especially the issues of martyrdom, world-hating, and overriding self-righteousness about God's plan and truth. For the Besht, the enlightened need neither evolution nor heaven because the future Messiah or the kingdom of God is right here and now playing in our hearts. There is no need to quest evolutionarily and heavenward because what we are seeking rests in the coals of the hearth in the home of our being.

This realization is not intellectual. Rather, it is playful, like playing with a riddle or a hide-and-seek game. It is full of paradox and humor because there is no need to seek. To continue thinking about the role of imagination, the concept of "as if," in religion, we need go no further than the Besht's parable about the King in the Palace. The Besht tells of a mighty king who built a great palace surrounded by walls and moats and wild beasts. The king then invited all the great men of the land and other realms to come visit him, ensconced in the fortified palace, promising rewards and riches to those who found him. Many came, enticed by the promise of riches, but all were deterred by the great dangers that stood between them and the king. It was only when the king's son came, guided by an intense love and desire to see his father, that the illusions of the palace fell away. There were no moats, no tigers, and no walls in reality—when awareness and love caused the illusions to disappear, the king was right there all along.[23]

Like the visitors who realize the king is already present—and in fact like the boy who discovers his friend is hiding in the tree right above him during a neighborhood game—the tzadik—the righteous seeker of Judaism—through a disciplined waiting for the Messiah, slowly is transformed by the realization that the Messiah has already arrived. With this realization the tzadik can actually heal and sanctify by envisioning our intrinsic wholeness and sanctity.

Jewish Philosophy

Jewish philosophers like Martin Buber drew inspiration from the example of the Besht's Hasidism. Buber found the ideal of conducting one's daily life in the full presence and consciousness of God to be a blueprint for all healthy relationships—the I–Thou relationship of mutual respect and recognition. For Buber, our whole life and humanity are defined by our relationship with the people and objects and ideas around us, engaging with others either as objects in an I–It relationship or as equals in an I–Thou relationship. In both cases, it is never just we alone who define our lives; it is the interaction *between* ourselves and the outward world. In the hyphen that links the I and the Thou, we form a spirit-oriented relationship in which domination and power fall away, leaving the engagement of hearts to hearts.

Buber wrote that this dynamic between one person and another is the "fundamental fact of human existence . . . which can be found nowhere [else] in nature."[24] This "between" experience is uniquely human and makes us different than anything else in nature. While this experience has many variations of quality and degrees of intensity, Buber wrote that it is "a primary quality of human reality. Man is made man by it."[25]

If Buber's terminology seems esoteric, it is nonetheless full of import for ego-transformation. It often occurs when we are engaged in a deep conversation with a friend and we are amazed by the shared compassion or unexpected insights. It can also simply be felt without any words, known through the "shared look" that touches each person deeply and sometimes overwhelms them, even to tears. We especially experience this "between" connection in intimate experiences. This intimacy could be lovemaking between spouses, deep conversation between friends, prayer between a person and God, breathtaking awe between hiker and nature, meditation between the no-longer-me and the not-yet-void, creative activity between artist and the possible, sports between team members and sometimes between opponents, and life-threatening combat among squad members. It can even be experienced by strangers who exchange a knowing look or experience a deeply shared sense of danger, relief, excitement, intuition, recognition, humor, or joy. Maybe at church. Maybe at a rock concert.

Buber's I–Thou state of mind evokes a deep recognition of the other—strangers or people otherwise outside our own tribe—in their fundamental humanity. Rather than seeing the other as an enemy or somehow radically different, it is as if we see them as a mother sees her son, as a wife feels for her husband, or as a father providing for, protecting, and playing with his child. Such a view would prevent us from seeing foreigners as inherently dangerous, or victims of police shootings as thugs, or refugees as so fundamentally different from us that they don't belong in our midst. Even in war there have been moments when combatants have been able to stop and recognize their fundamental shared humanity, such as when French, British, and German soldiers suspended hostilities to celebrate Christmas together during World War I. It is this ability to acknowledge a shared humanity that is required for ego-transformation.

CHRISTIANITY

Christianity too has its figures of play. In the ever-present tug-of-war between a dogmatic approach to religion and a relational approach, these Christian believers found in play a valuable vehicle for ego-transformation.

St. Francis of Assisi

In Andre Vauchez's biography of Francis (1181–1226), he writes of the saint's playful approach to Catholicism.[26] Francis was a fun-loving young aristocrat who became more and more attached to the poor, eventually renouncing his patrimony and dedicating himself to "Lady Poverty." He arranged the first live nativity scene in 1223 and was known for his love of animals, famously preaching to the birds. He traveled among poor communities and made the public "laugh at his own expense by presenting himself as a 'jongleur of God.'" During Francis's time, *jongleur* referred to people who were actors and narrators of stories, mimes, acrobats, and clowns, improvising comic skits to entertain their audiences. Jongleurs moved among the common people (unlike the troubadours who catered to lordly courts), performing for the marginalized, the vagrant, those who lived hand to mouth. They would deride the powerful with farce and dared to say what people actually thought of them.

Francis associated jest and fun with God, which was a provocative stance for his times. He effectively challenged the "traditional boundaries between the sacred and profane," arriving in a town as the knight of Lady Poverty and herald of the Great King, the poor and crucified man of Galilee. His antics held the attention of the delighted crowds but the church hierarchy was not always pleased. Church authorities were critical of jongleurs, who glorified popular military or legendary figures, and felt that Assisi risked putting scripture on the same level of fables.[27] Vauchez continues:

> Thus did the papacy endeavor, even during the lifetime of Francis and especially after his death, to restrict the right to preach only to the learned brothers and, after his death, to prohibit it to those who were not clerics, in both meanings of the terms, canonical and cultural. But in the eyes of the Poor Man of Assisi, these distinctions hardly made any sense, because the vocation of the Friars Minor was not, like solemn preachers, to sprinkle their sermons with sixty or eight Latin citations but to [share with them] their beliefs and experiences.[28]

It is Francis who, in his time, opened up the affective possibilities of Christ's good news to a church that had been dominated by rational or aesthetic concerns.[29]

Francis is considered one of the historical figures who followed Jesus most faithfully. Some called him "alter Christus"—another Christ—a type of play in itself in which one pretends to be the teacher or model one wishes to emulate, like a child who make-believes he is a famous sports hero. This kind of formative play bridges the gap between the real and the make-believe, the way things are and the possible, a kind of "fake it till you make it." Francis embodied participation, imagination, and in-betweenness, running all of them through with a sense of fun that eschewed proper pastoral teaching in favor of putting cows in with a manger and preaching to birds in the pews of their branches. This legacy continues today, as many Catholic and Anglican churches host a "Blessing of the Animals" on his feast day, October 4, where lines of churchgoers carrying their dogs and cats and ferrets and more can be found talking and laughing and awaiting their blessing.

Meister Eckhart

Meister Eckhart is another Christian who was unexpectedly taken with play. Eckhart was a German theologian who lived not long after Francis, from 1260 to 1328. Elaborating from scripture, Eckhart proposes his Christian interpretation: that the Trinity—Father, Son, and Holy Spirit—have played together eternally, before time and creation. He zeroes in on the Holy Spirit, identifying it as the "play between" Father and Son as well as play itself:

> This play was played eternally before all natures, As it is written in the Book of Wisdom, "Prior to creatures, in the eternal now, I have played before the Father in an eternal stillness." The Son has eternally been playing before the Father as the Father has before his Son. The playing of the twain is the Holy Ghost in whom they both disport themselves and he disports himself in both. Sport and players are the same. Their nature proceeding in itself. "God is a fountain flowing into itself," as St. Dionysius says.[30]

Eckhart's meditation is dazzling. Mystically, Eckhart intuits that God understands himself as eternal play. This is God's nature and consciousness—always has and always will be—and creation itself is God's play. Matthew Fox interprets Eckhart in this way: "Do you want to know what goes on in the core of the Trinity? I will tell you. In the core of the Trinity the Father laughs and gives birth to the Son. The Son laughs back at the Father and gives birth to the Spirit. The whole Trinity laughs and gives birth to us."[31]

Both Eckhart and the Hindu mystics hint that play is our eternal origin. Thinking of creation, of our very existence, in this way—as the play of God—may be unsettling. But our needless origin both humbles and frees us. We are an afterthought, the seepage of spirited play. But we are also the eternal play itself, and getting this, we are eternally free to play beyond a purpose-driven life that likens virtue to serious work, progress, security, and getting more. There is a joy in the freedom implied, a sense that fun is good in itself, and one that brings good as well. It is the laborious *trying* of prescriptive spirituality, of a religion of rules and directives, that impedes us. As Eckhart wrote, "If a man thinks he will get more of God by meditation, by devotion, by ecstasies, or by special infusion of grace than by the fireside or in the stable—that is nothing but taking God, wrapping a cloak round His head and shoving Him under a bench. For whoever seeks God in a special way gets the way but misses God."[32]

As noted earlier, the Judaic and Christian creation account is more *plan* than play. The Creator is active in his creation, often as a father-judge who instructs, comforts, and punishes wickedness. Creation is ordered by law, reason, seriousness, and hard work, with a heavy emphasis on loyalty and obedience. This idea of creation is dominant in Western religions, but Meister Eckhart's imagery of creation "boiling over" from the Trinity's play is an idea that is threaded through other Christian thinkers, from from St. Gregory to the advocates of process theology, not to mention Hinduism and even evolutionary philosophy. These speculations almost got him toasted by the church's earthly version of hell, but his writings managed to skip through history safely to offer us a uniquely playful vision of medieval Christian thought.

TANTRIC BUDDHISM

Karen Armstrong states,

> It is an arresting fact that right across the board, in every single one of the major world faiths, compassion . . . is not only the test of any true religiosity, it is also what will bring us into the presence of [God]. Why? Because in compassion, when we feel with the other, we dethrone ourselves from the center of our world and we put another person there. And once we get rid of ego, then we're ready to see the Divine."[33]

The Golden Rule itself originated in Southeast Asia, as Armstrong notes: The Golden Rule was "first propounded by Confucius five centuries before Christ: 'Do not do to others what you would not like them to do to you.'"

As Buddhism has gained a place in Western culture, its emphasis on compassion has appealed as much as its playful tendencies. From the practice of yoga to the figure of the Laughing Buddha to the beautiful art of sand mandalas, Buddhism has practices that have sacred origins and purposes but also offer an intriguing playfulness to those steeped in more somber traditions. Perhaps none more so than tantric Buddhism's sacred sex. Tantric Buddhism uses sexuality as a yogic practice, elevating the soul. The idea seems wild and experimental, so far removed from the ultraserious rituals of so many other religious practices. This perhaps explains the fascination that the West has had with tantra in recent years.

But the origin of tantric practices is less well known. Miranda Shaw explains how tantric Buddhism, which first emerged in the ninth century CE, was a departure from Buddhist monasticism and other ways of life that separated the holy from the everyday:

> The founders of tantra came from all walks of life. . . . The main impetus for the movement, though, did take place outside the monasteries, from what we would call laypeople—people who wanted to practice yoga and spiritual disciplines, but not necessarily in a monastic context as celibates, and not in separation from members of the opposite sex or outside of the context of their intimate and familial relationships.[34]

The tantric movement built on the inherent playfulness and freedom of Buddhism. Shaw continues:

> During the tantric period, we find Buddhism once again expanding its base and actually reaching out to people, for example, in the mountains, at the borders of society, and at the lower rungs of society. As these people entered Buddhism, they brought with them their own forms of spirituality, their own symbolism and ritual skills. . . . There was no central organizing or authorizing body that would censor the teachings in advance or would limit who could teach, which is one of the reasons why it was such a creative period.[35]

Tantra introduced new practices into Buddhism. This made Buddhism, more than ever, a participatory activity rather than simply a liturgical one—something you *did* rather than just something you showed up for, learned, or observed:

> The basic mindfulness techniques and ethical teachings of Buddhism were already in place by this time. What was added [with tantra] was the incorporation of a number of yogic techniques, specific ways of directing the breath and the inner energies of the body . . . as well as magical techniques and dance practices. Probably what was most distinctive about this period . . . was the introduction of the yoga of union—the practices that men and women could do together in order to transform the energies awakened by sexual union into very refined states of consciousness, wisdom and bliss.[36]

From this description it's evident that tantric Buddhism also celebrated fun and imagination as well. The acceptance of local practices, to opening the door to whatever diverse people might bring to the party, as well as the inclusion of activities such as sex and dancing reflect these playful values.

MYSTICISM

Although mysticism is not a religion unto itself, it constitutes such a distinct practice within otherwise orthodox belief—and such a unified practice across belief systems—that it deserves special mention. The mystical experience is surprisingly similar in all religious traditions through the ages, an adventure into mind-blowing contradictions, labyrinth-like paths blocked by imaginary monsters and devils and unendurable loneliness, a contest between soul and an unconquerable Spirit that is ultimately realized as deadly but not serious, prompting a laugh from the divine depths.

Mysticism—in all its variations across all religions—offers a fascinating juxtaposition of attributes, occupying the in-betweenness of play. Most often thought of as a meditative practice that brings the practitioner into an experience of the divine, mysticism allows us to experience a personal God with whom we might have an intimate experience (although personalization can have its problems[37]) as well as an impersonal God who is beyond human categories, beyond the personal, a force or energy similar to the physical forces of nature (which is reflected especially in Taoism). A personal God dialogues; an impersonal God is silent. The word of a personal God calls humanity to action; an impersonal God to the silence of the ineffable and unutterable through contemplation. At its extreme, it might even be considered as existing between life and death, as the mystic remains in this world but communes with God in a way that most of us imagine as only happening after death.

If mysticism reflects the in-betweenness of God as person and God as force, it also encompasses the imaginative aspect of play, not only in its practice but in attempts to express that practice to the outside world. Some say that the mystical journey, much less its realization, cannot be adequately put into language. When spoken or written about, it is either apophatic (expressed as meditative silence) or negative language that describes the ineffable in terms of what it is not. But another view considers art—including poetry, abstract imagery (e.g., Islam expression), iconography (e.g., Greek Orthodox), and music, which skirts the limits of rational thought—as a kind of play that offers up tantalizing moments of insight or even experience of the mystical moment.

The mystic relies on ambiguous terms—like play and Spirit—that defy definitional consensus. However, the muddy mush of mystical lingo with its appetite for overarching epiphenomena, zesty exaggerations, subversive contradictions, and poetic indulgences seems a suitable trough for play and Spirit. Mysticism likes epiphenomena, all-inclusive terms that to the rationalist are so broad and inclusive that they say nothing. They don't mind the jumbled attempts to convey their experience, recognizing that language can never fully capture what it is they are trying to point to. Ambiguity is a way of ironically honoring the ineffability of their interest and dedication.

Seen in the light of mysticism, the discrete personal God of religion is only a stage, a necessary fiction on the way to the ineffable. Play is the vehicle, appropriately outside the limitations of reason, that can recognize the images of the divine as real, then as reflections, and finally as illusory (and delusional) once one is realized or illuminated in, as, and through the Absolute. These mystics divine a Spirit masquerading as infinite forms, shape-shifting, welcoming the play of category but refusing to be categorized. It seems to relish the competitive naming games of philosophers and theologians, yet slips through their theoretical fingers as they realize they have no privileged seat at the feet of God. Sometimes this Spirit appears as the One, sometimes the Many. Sometimes it's the All, and sometimes nothing at all. At times it is an essential Being, and at others an eternal Becoming. Some think it to be a personal God; others, an impersonal Force. It is called Reason, Will, Higher Power, and Love and has been given incarnational status from avatars to Jesus. It takes on the shapes of ancestors and animal magic, the sun and rain, and gods and goddesses.

Play is the vehicle that the mystic drives and is driven in, both as playing driver and played passenger. The mystical experience is primal, universal, enchanting, transcending, requiring release, and engaging in profound relationship with a God who is playing hide-and-seek or who has a magic wand that can make him vanish—a God who like the make-believe fairest princess insists on the heroic effort of ego-annihilation as the price of her illuminating presence. For the proof of the mystical experience is in the transformation that follows.[38]

NEUROSCIENTISTS, NOVELISTS, AND OTHER PLAYFUL THINKERS

The twentieth and twenty-first century are full of thinkers who, while not quite theologians or priests or shamans, have thought deeply and ethically about spirituality. These include people as diverse as scientists, literary critics, and philosophers. Their insights open up new visions of the spiritual value of play.

Neuroscientists

One group of these thinkers are the neuroscientists who are setting out on adventures in mind and faith. The fun of spirituality was hinted at by Harvard psychiatrist George E. Vaillant in his book *Spiritual Evolution: A Scientific Defense of Faith*.[39] Connor Wood notes that Vaillant "lays out a fascinating argument: that spirituality has primarily to do with positive emotions such as joy, compassion, awe, and gratitude, and that during the course of human history these emotions have been, and continue to be, evolutionarily adaptive."[40] Vaillant explores the traits of faith, love, hope, joy, forgiveness, compassion, and awe and mystical illumination, showing how these traits contribute to our evolution and the process of ego-transformation.

His proof comes from some surprising sources. Vaillant cites studies of voles in which female voles are deprived of oxytocin, the "cuddle hormone." He writes, "If they are genetically deprived of oxytocin, monogamous, maternal, loving prairie voles (a species of rodent) turn into another subspecies—the heartless, promiscuous, pup-abusing montane voles. Without oxytocin, parental cooperation and responsibility vanish." Vaillant notes that the production of oxytocin coincides with everything from holding infants to teenage crushes to orgasm.[41] The same can be said of endorphins, a neurochemical associated with both kindness and thrill-seeking and other fun activities like skiing and playing board or video games.[42] These studies confirm what we intuit from history and personal experience: Fun is good for our souls.

Postmodernists

Postmodernists introduced a new idea—that all thought systems, from doctrines to science to religions to national narratives, are games, useful fictions that describe a particular view of reality, but not all of reality. For postmodernists, all ways of knowing are forms of play. Each way has its unique assumptions of what reality entails and specific rules that dictate how to access and understand the reality under question. We cannot access an absolute reality through our metanarratives—religious beliefs, national founding mythologies, and the like—because they constitute human-made stories that can only express part of our experience. Language itself is an "as if" expressive play grounded in idiosyncratic assumptions and prejudices.

Acknowledging the fictional basis of even our most treasured ideas and narratives need not lead us to a materialistic jadedness. If we can't know for sure that the earth was created in six days or that Mohammed literally went to the mountain, it's of no matter. We are human, we are limited, and we are humbled by our mortality and limited perspective. And it may be that, for us humans, making any connection with the divine is always preceded by pretending there is one. If this is an example of "fake it till you make it," faking it may be one of our highest spiritual paths.

CONCLUSION

Play turns out to have a surprisingly robust history and role in religion and spiritual thought, from the earliest Hindus to the latest neuroscientists. Along with love, it has been mystically and metaphorically attributed as the primal, preexisting, and unborn "process and content" of the Godhead or Absolute in both East and West. Long before creation, play was, we've imagined, the activity of the Godhead. These play forms included dreaming, painting with light, meditating, and potentiality. These are human myths, projections, not an assertion of metaphysical reality, more mythos than logos. But their universality suggests that play is primal, despite our contemporary view that play is secondary to work, reason, and seriousness.

These insights show us potential paths to ego-transformation. They allow us to take responsibility for our actions and the way we shape the world. They steer us away from rigidity and overcertainty, which so often lead to oppression rather than freedom. They let us see that all religions and philosophies are ultimately what Peter Berger called a merciful illusion, Friedrich Nietzsche an indispensable error, Hans Vaihinger a useful fiction, and my wife Ruth making stuff up.

But a spiritual journey rooted in play does not have to forever chase something out of grasp, does not have to refuse the comforts of conclusions or beliefs. The dance of certainty and doubt informs all approaches to play. Doubt plays out in the attitude of *hope*: Hope has to do with that which forever appears and forever recedes—in the rising and setting of the sun, the waxing and waning of the moon, the beginning and end of day and night, and in the construction and destruction of reality into the something better, with the flux of the play of becoming. Hope is what allows us to let go to the cycles of life, permitting us to imagine (but not require) a holy path. Hope is changeable and doubtful, making room for compassion and possibility.

Certainty plays out in the attitude of *faith:* Faith fixes its eye on a constant, immovable sun on the horizon, whether a sunrise or sunset, whether cloudy or cloudless, whether orange with blues or white with greys. Faith is constant, sure, and certain, giving us rest amid chaos and uncertainty. Faith attends to what seems secure so that play can unfold in some meaningful way—so that it can unfold not only as a creation but as something good and beautiful.

If faith is the pallet, the canvas, the frame, the oil, then hope is the brushstroke, the muscle movement, and the possibility of the good, true and beautiful. Hope has to do with becoming what can be, while faith has to do with being with what is, just as it is, with what play reveals. Hope yearns and seeks after what may become, with what is still hidden and unrevealed, while faith accepts and witnesses what is and has become.

Movement between the poles of hope and faith, certainty and doubt, and rigidity and freedom, constitute our path of spirituality. And as theologians and believers from the Besht to your neighborhood yoga teacher have shown, play is a beautiful metaphor for this path, one that encompasses both self-responsibility and divine joy.

NOTES

1. Karen Armstrong, "My Wish: The Charter for Compassion," TED Talk, https://en.tiny.ted.com/talks/karen_armstrong_makes_her_ted_prize_wish_the_charter_for_compassion

2. Joshua Wolf Shenk, "What Makes Us Happy?" *The Atlantic*, June 2009, https://www.theatlantic.com/magazine/archive/2009/06/what-makes-us-happy/307439/.

3. M. Wenner, "The Serious Need for Play," *Scientific American*, February 2009.

4. National Institute for Play, "The Vision," http://www.nifplay.org/vision/overview/

5. Michel de Montaigne, *The Essays: A Selection*, trans. M. A. Screech (New York: Penguin, 1993), 234.

6. Quoted in C. Barron, "Creativity and the Liminal Space," *Psychology Today*, June 4.

7. Jay Michaelson, "The Truth about Burning Man," *Huffington Post*, September 15, 2009, http://www.huffingtonpost.com/jay-michaelson/the-truth-about-burning-m_b_279464.html.

8. Kim Knott, *Hinduism: A Very Short Introduction* (Oxford: Oxford University Press, 1998), 117.

9. William S. Sax, "Introduction," in William S. Sax (ed.), *The Gods at Play: Lila in South Asia* (Oxford: Oxford University Press, 1995), 3–8.

10. Sax, "Introduction," 3–4.

11. Ram Shanker Misra, *The Integral Advaitism of Sri Aurobindo* (Motilal Banarsidass, 1998).

12. Misra, *Integral Advaitism of Sri Aurobindo*.

13. Sri Aurobindo, *The Life Divine* (Twin Lakes, WI: Lotus Press, 1990), 103.

14. Graham M. Schweig, *Dance of Divine Love: The Rasa Lila of Krishna* (Princeton, NJ: Princeton University Press, 2005).

15. Schweig, *Dance of Divine Love*.

16. Sax, "Introduction," 4.

17. Abby Ellin, "The Enlightened Path, with a Rubber Duck," *New York Times*, December 31, 2008.

18. Ellin, "The Enlightened Path."

19. Ellin, "The Enlightened Path."

20. Ellin, "The Enlightened Path."

21. Ellin, "The Enlightened Path."

22. Ketonet Passim (1866), 28a.

23. Yitzhak Buxbaum, *The Light and Fire of the Baal Shem Tov* (New York: Continuum, 2005).

24. Martin Buber, *Between Man and Man*, trans. Ronald Gregor-Smith (New York: Routledge Classics, 2002; orig. 1947), 240.

25. Buber, *Between Man and Man*.

26. Andre Vauchez, *Francis of Assisi: The Life and Afterlife of a Medieval Saint*, trans. Michael Cusato (New Haven, CT: Yale University Press, 2012), 321–322.

27. Vauchez, *Francis of Assisi*, 321–322.

28. Vauchez, *Francis of Assisi*, 322.

29. Vauchez, *Francis of Assisi*, 323.

30. Meister Eckhart, quoted in D. T. Suzuki, Mysticism: Christian and Buddhist (London: Allen & Unwin, 1957). See also F. Pfeiffer, *Meister Eckhart*, vol. 1, trans. C. Evans (London: John M. Watkins, 1924), 147–148.

31. Matthew Fox, *Meditations with Meister Eckhart* (Rochester, VT: Bear and Company, 1981).

32. Meister Eckhart, Pr. 16b, quoted in Joel Harrington, *Dangerous Mystic: Meister Eckhart's Path to the God Within* (New York: Penguin, 2018).

33. Armstrong, "My Wish: The Charter for Compassion."

34. Miranda Shaw, interview by Craig Hamilton, reprinted from *What Is Enlightenment?* magazine, Spring–Summer 1998.

35. Shaw, interview, 1998.

36. Shaw, interview, 1998.

37. Karen Armstrong, *The History of God* (New York: Ballantine, 1993), 210ff.

38. See Jerome Gellman, "Mysticism," *Stanford Encyclopedia of Philosophy*, https://plato.stanford.edu/entries/mysticism/#3. "Further enhancement of the validity of a religious or mystical experience can come from appropriate consequences in the life of the person who had the experience, such as increased saintliness."

39. George E. Vaillant, *Spiritual Evolution: A Scientific Defense of Faith* (New York: Harmony, 2008).

40. Connor Wood, "Vaillant on 'Spiritual Evolution,'" *Science on Religion* website, September 6, 2009, https://www.scienceonreligion.org/index.php/bookreviews/116-spiritual-evolution

41. George E. Vaillant, "The Neuroendocrine System and Stress, Emotions, Thoughts and Feelings," *Mens Sana Monographs* 9, no. 1 (2011): 113–128.

42. Nigel Mathers, "Compassion and the Science of Kindness: Harvard Davis Lecture 2015," *British Journal of General Practice* 66, no. 648 (2016): e525–e527, https://www.ncbi.nlm.nih.gov/pmc/articles/PMC4917056/. Kevan Lee, "Games and Your Brain," *Buffer* website, June 27, 2013, https://blog.bufferapp.com/brain-playing-games-why-our-brains-are-so-attracted-to-playing-games-the-science-of-gamification.

Chapter 6

Meditation
The Ultimate Play

I was raised Catholic and was a devout follower of Catholicism for many years. As I grew and studied, I found a spiritual home in Buddhism, specifically in its practice of meditation. Buddhism, for me, was a reprieve from the dogmatic specificity of Catholicism; meditation, a valuable tool for escaping egoism. I have practiced Zen Buddhist meditation for many, many years and have found in its practice a beautiful spirit of play. This chapter is my attempt at conveying the play of Buddhist spirituality.

Buddhism was founded by Gautama Buddha (also known as Siddhartha or simply the Buddha), who lived sometime around the fifth century BCE in India. The traditional story of his life is that he was a young prince shielded by his family from the suffering of the world. As a young man, he ventured into the world and, appalled by the existence of suffering and death, rejected worldly goods and became an ascetic. The ascetic life proved unfulfilling and wasteful to him, and he developed the idea of the Middle Way—striking a balance between sensual indulgence and rigid asceticism. As a Hindu, he sought an escape from *samsara*, the karmic cycle of birth, suffering, death, and rebirth in which humans were trapped, but he had yet to gain insight into how to be released from samsara. At thirty-five years old, he sat under a tree and declared he would not leave until he was granted enlightenment.

After forty-nine days of meditation, Gautama had the enlightenment that he sought, thereby gaining the name of Buddha, or enlightened one. This enlightenment was expressed as the Four Noble Truths—that life is suffering, that suffering comes from attachment (everything from desire and fear to attachment to a personal identity), that suffering can come to an end, and that the end of suffering (nirvana) is attained through the Noble Eightfold Path (encompassing such practices as right view, right speech, right conduct, and meditation). By understanding these insights and following this path, a person could attain liberation.

The Buddha was committed to help others attain nirvana, and he shared teachings that were passed down orally and then written down a few centuries after his death, writings known as the "sutras." The whole of his teaching is often referred to as "dharma," the path of rightness. Buddhism was centered in India until the first century CE, when it was first introduced in China and from where it spread elsewhere in Southeast Asia. In roughly the seventh century CE, a specific school of Buddhism—known as Zen Buddhism—developed in China during the Tang dynasty. Zen Buddhism was particularly focused on meditation and the bodhisattva ideal, with less emphasis on the sutras and doctrine. In fact, the term "Zen" derives from the Japanese pronunciation of *chan,* derived itself from the ancient Sanskrit word for meditation, "dhyana."

HOW MEDITATION BECOMES PLAY

Meditation in some form is a nearly universal practice. It is enshrined as breathing exercises, prayer, chanting, and a hundred other religious practices that share the same DNA: a place of quiet; a connection with what is real, underneath the chaos and particulars of everyday life; concentration; going beyond the self; and entering into an alternative form of consciousness. Zen meditation in particular involves concentrating on the breath, being aware of transience, and letting go of all that is transient: desire, anger, thoughts, rationality, even identity. Meditation is not a fight against these things, however, but a flanking move, a means of seeing and letting go rather than engaging.

But how do meditation and play connect? Any connection between play and spirituality must take into account meditation, because it is a universal spiritual practice. But play and meditation, like fire and water, seem at odds. Play sparks with fun while meditation cools with sedate seriousness. Play appears dynamic, interactive, even exuberant, while meditation seems quiet, inward, and peaceful. Play exudes activity and the relational; meditation, stillness and the solitary. Play reaches out, desires, and energizes, while meditation lets go, lets be, and calms.

Considering someone like the Dalai Lama makes us wonder. He, like many long-practicing meditators, has a happy, playful disposition. His smile is spacious, his laughter contagious. Obviously, positing a simple cause-and-effect relation between playfulness and meditation cannot be supported. Joyful temperaments and optimistic views could explain this playfulness as well, and some dedicated meditators can be downright somber folks. But people like the Dalai Lama makes us think that fire and water can combine to make a little holy steam.

So how do the two connect? What makes play an apt metaphor for Zen spirituality?

Participation

To start with, play and meditation both require participation. All play begins with intention, whether we're playing a game, doing a creative activity, playing a sport, making love, or meditating. This is true even with frivolous play. Overcoming the inertia of a lounge chair and joining a volleyball game takes some effort and a tad bit of commitment, even if it's just to risk looking foolish when you dive for that well-placed spike. At the other end of the play spectrum are professional athletes, entertainers, and artists, whose disciplined effort and dedication are their daily bread. All play is colored with more or less serious goals, effort, and commitment.

Bringing goals into the picture may seem contradictory to the nature of play (and meditation) that we laid out previously. Play is inherently autotelic, being an end in itself. Therefore having a goal can sabotage spontaneous fun and the unfolding of enlightenment. The joy of play and enlightenment can become infected by a controlling, driven, and goal-oriented ego. We can be attached to a specific goal like winning or avoiding humiliation. This is a recipe for disaster because stuff happens that we can't control. Because of this, narrow and rigid goals can derail us and undermine our intent. But the broad goals of fun and joy are intrinsic to play and will survive change, broken plans, new limitations, and newly opened doors. Perhaps *effort* is a better word than *goal*.

So too with meditation. Meditation may help lower blood pressure or promote relaxation for twenty minutes, but only a sustained effort keeps it so. This is especially true when the goal is enlightenment. For most, this goal takes a lifetime—perhaps many lifetimes. The obstacles are many and guaranteed. Commitment means taking instruction, following the rules, and embracing meditation's challenges, while effort means getting out of our chairs and doing the work. Comparisons between meditation and sports are common, and for good reason. Sports can be fun but require sometimes tedious training before an athlete can achieve the mastery that allows the fun. In meditation, the human body is the playing field, and attention is the skill that is being mastered. Participation, intention, and dedication, these are things that draw us into ever deeper levels of play *and* spirituality.

Fun

With goals set and commitments made—and with time and effort—we slide into a different world. In play and meditation, the everyday world is left behind. Roles, expectations, and duties vaporize as we become lighter in this free world. We become golfers-no-longer-attorneys, writers-no-longer-housewives, and meditators-no-longer-psychologists. We become seekers of the really real. Day jobs are left behind, except for the fortunate few whose work is their play.

The play experience is an altered state driven by fast-acting, feel-good drugs produced by our bodies and souls. Notice how quickly playing hide-and-seek with a four-year-old transports us, when only moments before we were wracked with worry about an upcoming mortgage payment. The naturally produced drugs of play make us forget. Serious one minute, goofy the next. These biochemicals lift us as they calm, energize us as they ease our worries. Perhaps drug addicts seek the same mind-altered state, not realizing that play can give a similar high without the downside. Maybe addiction is a play-deprived illness.

Meditation has been shown to likewise have powerful psychological benefits.[1] Although meditators are more likely to call the feeling "bliss" or "joy" than "fun," a powerful positive emotion draws us back to the play of meditation again and again. Erik Erikson famously wrote, "The playing adult steps sideward into another reality."[2] As in everyday play, in meditation we indeed step sideward into a different reality where "thinking" is set aside, detached observation of oneself and the world replace it, one's egoic functioning wanes, and the novel experiences of calm and joy arise spontaneously.

These feelings of joy are not immediate; they require our participation. When we first sit and allow our mind to just be, we notice the buzz of thoughts, sensations, feelings, and images in our heads. Without fighting it but by letting this buzz go without trying to repress or change it, it soon evaporates, leaving a deeper stillness. The Zen student sits quietly and allows the play of his mind and body to take place without interfering. There is no seeking some special pleasure or experience; rather meditation takes this reality just as it is without seeking any particular outcome. The paradox is that relinquishing any particular outcome to meditation, when practiced well, generates an immense sense of joy and peace.

Meditation writ large—including prayer—sometimes includes a playmate, another player whom we become aware of and get to know as the most sublime part of the play. We see this in Hindu, Muslim, Christian, Jewish, and Neoplatonic mysticism. Buddhist meditation, including Vipassana and Zen, has no personal God with whom to play. This meditation is limited to the mind's debris, thoughts and mundane phenomena that ceaselessly bob up and down on the waves of consciousness. And further still, in deep meditation one detaches from this flotsam and even the self that notices it.

Meditators see an ocean of play all around them. Its water rises into clouds and falls as rain. Nothing is permanent, life constantly changes. The play of the seasons of life: the soil with ceaseless heat and moisture; sun and rain that nurture and destroy in ceaseless cycles. The meditator becomes as absorbed as an athlete running down a field with the wind on his face or a writer losing track of the hours as she thinks, composes, rewrites, and sees new revelations that let her think, compose, and rewrite all anew. It is *flow* at the deepest level.

Imagination

Play unleashes new perspectives about the way things are or might be. It revels in uncertainty, unlike our workaday world, inviting twists and turns, flip-flops and surprises. What seems to be is not always what is. Upsets occur. Paradox reigns. Read any novel and be surprised by sudden turns of events. The muses of creative activity take us to places we had no intention visiting.

So with meditation. The altered state of consciousness that comes with deep meditation opens up new worlds of insight and feeling. We come to understand that fiction can be truer than fact, that the imagination sees deeper than reason, and that letting go is a power without a grasp. Here, a timeless now has no time zone; it eternally vibrates the same second everywhere.[3] In play, we come to understand that the present is all there is, that our views of reality are fantasies, and that unintended joy is both the purpose of play and of life itself.

Zen meditation shares with mysticism a "do it yourself" approach to spirituality. Rather than taking a long historical journey back to origins, relying on experts and sages to guide the way, the meditator finds that access is immediate and authenticated by the experience itself. It is authenticated by the meditator, not by authorities, doctrines, or myths, all of which are open to question and individual interpretation and misuse. This is what the mystics did in various ways: whether they contemplated divine mysteries or deities, engaged the infinite regress, recited mantras, emptied their selves of egoic pleasures, or gave themselves through compassionate service. Discovery and creation trump doctrines, methods, and rules.

Liminality

The play experience transforms. Our whole being, body, mind, and spirit, becomes engaged. Slowly, the self that initiated the play recedes; we stop thinking about ourselves and start thinking of the play. Self-consciousness eases into a play consciousness that bubbles with freedom and spontaneity.

This journey from one state to another, from me-centered to reality-centered, is the heart of meditation. When we meditate, the mind is like a playground, where rambunctious children tirelessly run, jump, climb, tag, giggle, shriek, hide, seek, spin, and do somersaults with no one in charge. Thoughts can be like a howling monkey who swings aimlessly through trees, jumps up and down, distracts our concentration, and demands we pay attention to its antics. This ceaseless and often purposeless play is the first experience of the meditative mind.

Our response is equanimity—to calmly not react to the mind's shenanigans. Elisha Goldstein in *The Now Effect* talks about the "space" where we find mindfulness—the space between stimulus and response.[4] Being in between what we perceive and how we react is where the meat of meditation is. It starts with awareness, and it ends with equanimity; in between those is where the play happens. And it is this space that Goldstein urges us to dwell in longer.

Many meditators shift focus to a mantra or sacred image. Some attend to the in-and-out passage of breath near the tip of their nose. Others systematically scan their body and notice its ever-changing sensations, while others (like those who practice Zen) just sit calmly with detached awareness and allow the never-ending play of the mind's monkeys unfold. By being nonreactive to its antics not fighting it, letting it be without judgmentthe intensity of the movement subsides, and we enter a deeper play.

In this way, meditation works like a flanking maneuver. The Buddhists' "skillful means" and "creative playfulness" offer, like AA, a no-shortcuts, slow, gradual, sustained practical means of developing mindfulness of the sensations that surround all cravings. Developing generosity, gratitude (which communicates to the self "I have enough" and stops the craving), and nonjudgmental awareness (avoiding labels like "alcoholic," "sinner," and "weakling"), often combined with ethical and communal supports, constitutes a shared platform for both practices. And the daily attendance to these develops discipline in mind and body.

The disciplined mind becomes aware of an ever-changing flow, a ceaseless rising and falling away of phenomenon, like the ebb-and-tide or the up-and-down white caps of an ocean, the figures in clouds, or the ripples in a brook. It's a struggle to put this play into a conceptual bucket, when it is more vast than an ocean. This play cannot be accommodated in the container of thought, because it is at once an ocean, water itself, and everywhere wetness that is both wet and dry and neither. The liminality of meditation is in both the state of the meditator and the state of the reality that he or she enters.

HOW MEDITATION BIRTHS EGO-TRANSFORMATION

As we've seen, the end goal of any spiritual practice is not mastery of the practice but transformation of the self. Zen Buddhism is no different. My practice has been Vipassana meditation, in which focused observation of the breath brings us in touch with change and impermanence. In addition, I practice *metta bhavana*. Sharon Salzberg describes the difference between Vipassana (an open monitoring meditation) and metta (a focused attention meditation) this way. While Vipassana is a practice of being aware of one's self, sensations, and surroundings, "in metta meditation, we direct lovingkindness toward ourselves and then, in a sequence of expansion, towards somebody we love already. Somebody we are neutral towards. Somebody we have difficulty with. And ultimately toward all beings everywhere without distinction."[5]

Giving oneself over to thoughts of lovingkindness, even to those one feels hostility for, is a transforming experience. It primes us to interact in the world with compassion, no matter what the circumstance or antagonist. Salzberg continues: "In contrast to Vipassana [which is principally an exercise in observation], in metta practice you are not focusing on the ultimate nature of phenomena. Furthermore, you are choosing a particular object of meditation, which is the metta phrase, such as 'May I be happy.'"[6] The metta phrase is then expanded outward in concentric circles: May my spouse be happy. May my coworker be happy. May my enemy be happy. May all the world be happy.

Robert Thurman writes about how meditation stimulates compassion.[7] The purpose of meditation is true enlightenment, not just for one's self but for the "team"—all sentient beings. Of course, when seeking the benefit of others' enlightenment, the first person who is benefited is yourself. It is a "wise selfishness"—by merely wanting others to be happy, you make yourself happy! In addition, when we let go of our own illusionary grasping and protecting of our self-interests and needs, and we give our time, energy, and resources to others, then we become truly blissful, truly and deeply happy. We then see that bliss is what binds the universes—large and small—together.

Thurman called this the *Bliss-Void Indivisible*. We let go, release, and let fall away the delusion of our separateness and individuality, as well as our (perceived) need to preserve and protect ourselves. Then we experience an incomparable happiness, the goal of all religions, especially Buddhism. This goes against the common preconception that we must endure a state of being semi-miserable in life—that life is painful, difficult, tedious, and inconsequential; that happiness is suspect, transient, and immature; and that death is a horrible, fearful end to the whole affair.

The bliss goes hand in hand with the void. The letting go of illusions of permanence and separateness takes place within the "between" of meditation and metta, which occur between worldly reality and transcendent reality. While metta engages compassion, Vipassana allows us to empty ourselves of illusions and ambitions. Strange as it seems, *emptiness* is the key connection between meditation and compassionate, loving action. It is the emptying—the kenosis of the ego's self-serving grasping, ignoring, and avoiding—that is the common element in meditation and compassionate action. This is the "great play," the great game worth playing, the great, skillful means to enlightenment. We empty our illusions of a separate self; we empty our self-serving interests in favor of serving and caring for others. We give over our effort, time, and concern to the good of others, *and* we give over our fear of dissolving, evaporating into an annihilating void.

Brain science has provided insights into the issues of ego and selflessness (see the appendix). But we also see moments of this all around us in day-to-day life. An athlete has an inkling of this deep motivation and experience when she "leaves it all on the field," when he "gives it his all," or when she "takes one for the team." It's easy to see why teams often get together for a common prayer at the end of a game—sport has long been a fertile ground for self-transcendence. Likewise an artist glimpses this emptying when he sets aside his comfort and commits his time and effort to the discipline of his art, when she takes a risk and expresses herself through a different art form, when he dedicates himself to learning new techniques and styles, when she opens and steps out of her comfort zone and exposes herself to creative forces that bubble up within her. A peace worker tirelessly empties himself and welcomes chances to make little pockets of peace for the oppressed, the hungry, and the marginalized.

The concepts of Buddhism are sometimes confusing to Westerners, and the use of terminology such as emptiness, void, and impermanence can seem, well, empty of meaning to them. In reality these terms connect metaphysics with ethics, and they point toward the universality of ego-transformation across all religions. The Buddhist empties himself of ego, the Hasidic Jew nullifies the ego through mystical prayer, and the Christian dies to himself to become one with Christ. In all these traditions, the seeker simultaneously lets go of self and gives of himself to others.

THE BODHISATTVA IDEAL

In the list of great players in the world—a list that might include Jesus, Gandhi, and Buddha—the ideal of the bodhisattva stands out to me. The bodhisattva is a figure in Hindu cosmology who, having come to the edge of nirvana, allows him- or herself to reenter the wheel of karma, returning again and again to the world in all sorts of forms to assist others in gaining enlightenment. The bodhisattva vow is to delay entering nirvana until all sentient beings have arrived there. The bodhisattva undertakes this "mission impossible" out of the transformation in emptiness that opens the player to lovingkindness and compassion as the natural disposition of play in the world.

How Enlightenment Leads to Emptiness

Buddhism asserts that the enlightenment comes by learning the Four Noble Truths: that life is suffering, that suffering comes from attachment, that suffering can be ended by practicing nonattachment, and that practicing nonattachment is done by following the Eightfold Path. The Eightfold Path consists of various mental disciplines, most notably the practice of meditation.

In this worldview, enlightenment leads to emptiness. But what exactly is emptiness? Emptiness is the state of nonattachment. It is what is left when the ego is cleared, when desire has been extinguished, and when the acquisitive disposition based on the sense of lack is given up. Bodhisattvas don't engage in a Manichean struggle between the forces of good and evil. Instead, by simply contemplating reality just as it is, they become enlightened about the transience of goods, attachments, desires, and fears and about the oneness of all beings.

How Emptiness Leads to Compassion

The bodhisattva finds the source of compassion in the emptiness that arises from enlightenment. But why do lovingkindness and compassion arise from emptiness?

The connecting piece between emptiness and compassion is meditation. Like a hyphen that joins two terms, like the liminal space of play, meditation sits between them, doing its mystical work, joining the life of the mind with the life of the world, the inner and the outer, the self and others.

Meditation is what allows us to be constantly aware of the true nature of reality. As expressed by the eighth-century Buddhist from India Kamalasila, "We should awaken the wisdom that comes from meditation so as to directly experience reality ourselves. All the teachings emphasize that even by much study and much consideration one cannot experience reality directly.... One who wishes to see reality face-to-face should set out to meditate."[8] Through meditation, our subconscious fears and motivations bubble to the surface, there to be acknowledged and dismissed. We are reminded of the transience of the world, the oneness of all beings, and the source of suffering—attachment. The fading sense of a separate self permits a knowing of our profound interconnectedness in the play of consciousness. This is not dogma but the experience of meditators time and time again.

The constant dwelling in these truths makes meditation a major league form of play. In meditation the realization arises spontaneously that we are profoundly interconnected to one another, that we cannot play without one another, and that we share through meditative awareness the same ground of consciousness. This gives rise to a natural compassion that does not rely on commandments or dogma but arises from the experience of our oneness and the gradual emptying out, day after day, of our egoic desires. As the meditator is immersed daily in the experience of compassion, the choice of evil simply drops out of their consciousness. Just like the flanking maneuver of AA, here there is no war on evil, no protestations against sin and human depravity, no urgency to fight for truth and justice, no need to proselytize; there is only the consciousness of compassion that arises from their enlightened vision and ongoing practice.

Sam Harris writes, "Once the selflessness of consciousness has been glimpsed [through meditation], spiritual life can be viewed as a matter of freeing one's attention more and more so that this recognition can become stabilized. This is where the connection between spirituality and ethics becomes inescapable."[9] As we practice the metta meditation, sending thoughts of lovingkindness in outward circles to those we love, those we are neutral about, those whom we don't like, and finally to all humanity and all sentient beings, we are being trained in the mentality of ethics and compassion.

How Compassion Leads to Ethical Behavior

Lovingkindness is what Buddhist enlightenment is all about, including for oneself. Bodhisattvas don't dwell on their mistakes; they start over again, getting better at what they do. We, unlike the enlightened bodhisattva, spend entirely too much time on our faults and shortcomings. We wade in the muck of our fallenness instead of moving on and rededicating ourselves to our original focus. We spend our time and energy on self-degradation instead of rectifying our mistakes, making amends and adjustments, and getting back to playing well. We don't laugh at ourselves; rather we toil in our own self-made seriousness. Instead of living with glee, we deaden ourselves with guilt. These emotions and judgments simply enmesh us further in attachments that meditation is meant to help us let go of.

Of course, ethics is not meant to stop with ourselves. Ethical behavior is both the result of ego-transformation and an impetus that facilitates ego-transformation. Having children, a cause, and a meaning beyond our immediate and selfish needs gives us the opportunity to serve others, to realize through direct experience that which is utterly beyond our everyday consciousness. The bodhisattva vow, recited by all who intend to follow the bodhisattva path, promises devotion to a series of "perfections" such as giving and patience, and the various obstacles to the vow are renounced, such as killing, boasting, and belittling others.

The bodhisattva vow is based on the beauty of compassion expressed in ethical behavior. This ethical behavior is rooted in many of the dynamics of play that we have noted before: It is the fruit of participation, of recognizing the other as a co-player. The bodhisattva vow allows one to influence others and also to be constantly influenced oneself. There is a disposition to openness to give and receive, to engage fully in the intrinsic interactive and relational quality of the play of play. The enlightened person is not simply trying to get everyone to share in the Spirit's joyful beauty but also to open himself to being influenced by the play that arises from others' experiences and ideas. Likewise the vow is a matter of dedication and practice. A vow or oath is meant to establish clarity and certainty in human relationships. It is meant to exclude lying, trickery, distortions, and fantastic elaborations in social relationships. The vow is a statement of clear resolve of the highest integrity and a commitment to practice.

What arises from this commitment is the fullness of beauty, the sense that what is beautiful is not acquisitiveness but a full outpouring of what arises without reservation, abundantly, gratuitously, and resplendently. The bodhisattva path is an aesthetic path, engaging with the beautiful. Care is beautiful. Lovingkindness is beautiful. Compassion is beautiful. Graciousness, hospitality, and generosity are beautiful.

And it is these things that the bodhisattva is dedicated to helping all beings experience. Like Jesus' urging of his disciples to love "the least of these," to visit those in prison and sit down to dine with the most hated people in society (then, as now, the tax collectors), the bodhisattva vows to help even the worst of the worst, for as long as it takes, for as many lifetimes as are required. The famous bodhisattva Kishitigarbha pledged to help even those "below" the status of humans: Kishitigarbha had

> a deep relationship with beings of the earth—humans, and especially with those 'below' it—the hungry ghosts and hell beings. Because these are the most difficult to raise into a more fortunate condition due to their previous unwholesome actions, and because of his past vow to save them all, Kishitigarbha has been known as the Teacher of the Dark Regions. 'If I do not go to hell to help them, who else will go?' is the famous declaration popularly attributed to Kishitigarbha. No matter what the crime or the karma, he is willing to have a connection with any being and to help free them from suffering.[10]

Like the Christ who gave up power and dominion on earth to suffer and save others, or like the character Katow in Andre Malraux's *Man's Fate* who, in the face of certain torture, gives up his cyanide tablet to another prisoner who fears a painful death, the bodhisattva forgoes his own comfort in order to help others escape the suffering of samsara. The bodhisattva ideal entails such practices as the "transfer of merit" (from one's own good deeds to others who may need it, including, for example, deceased relatives) and upaya, or "skillful means" that help others realize enlightenment.

The bodhisattva ideal and upaya are two of the ways that Buddhists pursue the goal of ego-transformation. As in all other traditions, serving others, even at the expense of one's own comfort or well-being, is the purpose of all we do. A central figure in Vipassana Buddhism, S. N. Goenka, wrote about the meaning of true compassion:

> It is the wish to serve people, to help them out of suffering. But it must be without attachment. If you start crying over the suffering of others, you only make yourself unhappy. . . . If you have true compassion, then with all possible love you try to help others to the best of your ability. If you fail, you smile and try another way to help. You serve without worrying about the results of your service. This is real compassion, proceeding from a balanced mind.[11]

CONCLUSION

Ethical behavior is the heart of every spiritual tradition, from the Golden Rule to the bodhisattva vow. Roger Walsh, in his *Essential Spirituality,* describes the elements that any serious spiritual practice must contain, such as reducing craving, doing good, being generous, and seeing the sacred in all things.[12] Nearly every tradition urges a combination of mental cultivation (e.g., reducing cravings) and ethical behavior (serving others), and in them all, a form of meditation is what links these two grand purposes.

NOTES

1. Richard Davidson, *The Emotional Life of Your Brain* (New York: Avery, 2012); Stephen S. Hall, "Is Buddhism Good for Your Health?" *New York Times*, September 14, 2003; Dan Gilgoff, "Can Meditation Change Your Brain? Contemplative Neuroscientists Believe It Can," *CNN's* Belief Blog, October 26, 2010; Hugh Delehanty, "The Science of Meditation," December 13, 2017, https://www.mindful.org/meditators-under-the-microscope/; Daniel Goleman and Richard Davidson, *Altered Traits: Science Reveals How Meditation Changes Your Mind, Brain, and Body* (New York: Avery, 2017).

2. Erik Erikson, *Childhood and Society*, 2nd ed. (New York: Norton, 1963), 222.

3. As Peter Berger writes, "In playing, one steps out of one time into another. . . . Joy is play's intention. When this intention is actually realized, in joyful play, the time structure of the playful universe takes on a very specific quality—namely, it becomes *eternity*." Peter Berger, *A Rumor of Angels* (New York: Anchor-Doubleday, 1990), 65–66.

4. Elisha Goldstein, *The Now Effect: How a Mindful Moment Can Change the Rest of Your Life* (New York: Atria, 2012).

5. Sharon Salzberg, "What is Metta Meditation? Discovering Your Capacity for Lovingkindness," *Tricycle*, https://tricycle.org/magazine/metta-practice/, reprinted

from Jean Smith (ed.), *Radiant Mind: Essential Buddhist Teachings and Texts—A Tricycle Book* (New York: Riverhead Trade, 1999).

6. Salzberg, "What Is Metta Meditation?"

7. This section from Robert Thurman, *Liberation upon Hearing in the Between: Living with the Tibetan Book of the Dead* (Boulder, CO: Sounds True Audio CD, 2005).

8. Stephan Beyer, ed. and trans., *The Buddhist Experience: Sources and Interpretations* (Belmont, CA: Wadsworth, 1974).

9. Sam Harris, *The End of Faith: Religion, Terror, and the Future of Reason* (New York: Norton, 2004), 219.

10. Yih-Mei Guo, trans., *The Bodhisattva Kishitigarbha Vow Sutra* (published by Yih-Mei Guo, 1997), https://www.beezone.com/BodhisvattaVow/BodhisattvaVow.html.

11. S. N. Goenka, in William Hart, *The Art of Living: Vipassana Meditation Taught by S. N. Goenka* (Onalaska, WA: Vipassana Resarch Publications, 1987), 124.

12. Roger Walsh, *Essential Spirituality: The Seven Central Practices to Awaken Heart and Mind* (New York: Wiley, 1999).

Chapter 7

Conclusion

"My heart leaps up when I behold, A rainbow in the sky: So was it when my life began, So it is now I am a man, So be it when I shall grow old. Or let me die! The child is the father of the man; And I could wish my days to be, Bound each to each by natural piety."

—William Wordsworth, "My Heart Leaps Up"

The child that we were, the child that we still have inside of us, has given our adult selves a gift. This gift is the experience and memory of play. As children, by playing we learn to cooperate, to include others, to find rules that are fair, to invest in projects until they are complete and make sense, and to develop a sense of pride and self-worth. We find joy, including the joy of self-forgetfulness, in which our childish (but often profound) worries and self-consciousness dissolve. Play is the thing kids most want to do, and when they are allowed, it becomes a bedrock of their happiness and mental health for years to come.

Our need for play is reflected in the joy that adults take in being "allowed" to participate in fun with their children or grandchildren. Pretending to be animals, playing patty-cake, hide-and-seek, our inner child glories in the chance to play at these things when we have the excuse of doing it for the children. We continue to love play as adults, when we permit ourselves to engage.

Clearly play has great value, but an interesting aspect is its surrender, its release to allow something other to take its place. It snips extraneous neuropathways for more efficient functioning in kids; it allows its free form to be folded into organized games; it permits itself to be a tool to be discarded once a problem is solved, a group is united, a game is won or lost, or an art form is expressed. Yet it is always there, waiting to be used yet again.

But just as, in Buddhist wisdom, a raft used to cross a river is discarded once the traveler reaches the other shore, and "skillful means" are used to convey truths about enlightenment until a seeker is able to grasp these truths more directly, play as an everyday activity can take us only so far. In this volume I've attempted to describe spirituality as a kind of play, and like all forms of spirituality, the end point is not the activity itself but the profound experience of self-transformation.

Play is powerful as a spiritual metaphor. It embraces the wide and wild diversity of religious views. It mimics the "free play" of postmodernism, whose essence is that we are all "making things up" and creating our own reality. It allows the freedom and fun of a global village where everyone has a chance to contribute or subvert the game, because the playing field of global communication is so wide and open. It makes room for the kind of uncertainty that is inescapable in today's world, offering an alternative to both fundamentalism and cynicism—an "as if" mentality that allows us to follow devoutly a path without needing to rigidly defend its absolute truth. It is a metaphor that offers meaning to suffering and great loss as well as hope and possibility for an evolving world.

Often in the past play was relegated to something tangential, even dangerous, or it was seen as an excuse for self-indulgence. When attempts to make play a philosophical or spiritual metaphor were made, the results were mixed. Emerson, Thoreau, and the other transcendentalists emphasized a personal freedom "from" the established dogma and rituals of the day, release from rigid, authoritarian, antiquated religious irrelevancies—a worthy cause but lacking a direction "to" something. In the 1960s the activists of play framed freedom only as egocentric rebellion, and fun only as pleasure. And the advocates of play in the great monotheistic religions (such as the Besht or Meister Eckhart) ended up as important but minority voices in their traditions.

It is time to revive the idea of play in spirituality, not as an escape but as a powerful spiritual and ethical activity that gives meaning without dogma, liberation through letting go of certainties, an alternative to both strict reason and wild indulgence.

PLAYING WITH THE DIVINE

Inherent in all religious belief and practice is an imaginative projection of hopes and dreams to the possibility of the Divine. Karen Armstrong posits that religion is a matter of imagination.[1] And Joseph Campbell saw play as being behind all myth, as the basis of wonder and the engine for humanity's imagining of the sacred.[2] What if we were to begin with this fundamental, universal, and ceaseless yearning to somehow connect to a (possibly make-believe) Divine Spirit through which meaning and purpose come into our lives? After all, while there may be an experience beyond words of the sacred, especially in the mystical traditions, when we try to put this into words all we are doing is making stuff up—using our insufficient words and insufficient ideas to capture that universal yearning for God.

All play in a religious sense seems to begin with common people's rituals, celebrations with music and dancing (like the ecstatic rituals described by Karen Armstrong and Barbara Ehrenreich). In these efforts to grasp something greater, we humans created myths that became theologies, stories that became philosophies, and we dignified these creations with an aggrandized status. As religion went from oral to written expression, from loose and egalitarian to organized and hierarchical, these stories and images became increasingly solidified and moved emphasis from free movement to consolidation, from loose interpretation to codification and dogma, from speculation to rationality, from "making things up" to facticity, and from truthfulness to Truth.

Indeed, the structures of the very institutions that codified these initial speculations are themselves made up—that is, created for the purposes of aiding both its members and perpetuating its own life—but end up reinforcing, sometimes violently, their supposedly factual status. These creations and their lawful codification were necessary to ground belief and control the chaos of followers of religious thought, but they also set in motion an "us versus you" mentality, a move from the play of speculative creativity to the play of side-taking competition, and from the participatory freedom of play to the dark dynamic of compulsion.

Once in place, these beliefs take on the status of a *given*, as the place where reality starts. We are given these assumptions as children and believe in their truth and goodness with little question. We feel they are objective, universal, unchangeable, and constant. This was what we inherited from Plato who thought there were universal Forms from which all proceeded or from Aristotle who thought there was an underlying being or truth that was a priori set in stone upon which all reality and knowledge could find firm foundation. These beliefs were constructed by men who viewed reality in terms of hierarchy and power, who assumed that reality needed to be rooted in some final, unchanging, universal, certain, and basic ground or being. They made this up because it seemed right, it had explanatory power, and it offered an understanding of the world. It was easy to then jump to the notion that this given was good, true, and beautiful.

It seemed to work for two millennia. The given of Christianity and the other great religions were some of humankind's most honored and trusted of useful fictions. God was on his throne and all was right with the world. But there were hidden problems with this false certainty. It rank-ordered who and what were important and had value and left those not privileged at the lower rungs of reality's ladder. Women, pagans, the poor and disenfranchised, and marginal thinkers were ranked low and attempts to raise them were often brutally suppressed. The structures of greed and power attached themselves to religion. Once attached, they could appropriate the given-ness of religion for themselves, brooking no doubt, no challenge. To doubt these structures of power, to oppose them at all, was a matter of heresy, an affront to God himself.

Becoming attuned to reality in all its diversity meant that the givens that had seemed essential to our civilization—to our very humanity—for so long were no longer reliable. But is it possible to find a new kind of given, based not on beliefs per se but on *values*? If so, what values can we identify that give us a grounding, a solid and even playing field, for our lives—and steer us away from our tendency to convert our aspirations into game and competition, with a win-all attitude that juices the balls and alters the field to our advantage? As this volume has argued, the metaphor of play gives us a useful direction.

THE PLAY

Embracing belief as play means the death of the given. This can be a frightening prospect. As postmodernism took a sledgehammer to the great stories that upheld our civilizations for millennia, the full consequences of the wreckage began to make themselves clear. For centuries humans have counted few things as certain as the process and facts of the scientific method, but thinkers like Paul Feyerabend, Friedrich Nietzsche, and Spariosu found cracks in the foundation of scientific certainty.[3] Linguists uncovered the way the meaning of words and narratives was malleable, and literary theorists like Roland Barthes found similar patterns in semiotics. We saw that we ourselves are in some ways "made up." We are socially constructed and unconsciously influenced by all sorts of social and cultural dispositions and movements that remain largely out of our sphere of awareness. We are "played by the larger culture" in this way and are unsettled by the realization. We fear also that we will lose some of the beauty and virtues that those great stories generated. Although their enmeshment with power structures produced often tragic outcomes, the great stories were also the fount of morality, of fine sensibilities, of beauty. They were the depository of our aspirations, our best instincts, our deepest yearnings for God, and our most loving impulses toward other human beings.

But losing these virtues altogether in cynical relativism or running back desperately to an antiquated fundamentalism are not our only choices. *Play* is a choice. We can create art, debate theology, imagine what God might be, and imagine what *we* might be, with all the potentially subversive, hopeful options they suggest. We create myths and mathematics and science. We devise structures to explain reality, a reality that is ceaselessly under construction. And all the while *acknowledge freely that this is what we're doing.*

This is human genius; this is our special ability. We are truly proficient at creating workable realities that continually are under revision, continually modified and redacted, for something better, some better way, some better explanation, some better idea. We can fully embrace the profound and humble realization that we really don't know, that we are saturated with uncertainty, but that we want to make ourselves, others, and our world better. It puts us all in the category of searching speculators, assigns us to practical solutions, and removes us from the grandiosity of having the truth and the limitations that "having the truth" entail. Making things up doesn't equal atheism or nihilism. Rather it acknowledges our limitations and even celebrates them.

John Shelby Spong, a former Episcopal bishop, wrote, "God is not a Christian, God is not a Jew, or a Muslim, or a Hindu, or a Buddhist. All of those are human systems which human beings have created to try to help us walk into the mystery of God. I honor my tradition, I walk through my tradition, but I don't think my tradition defines God, I think it only points me to God." This is the core of what we wryly call "making things up."

I once counseled a woman who had gone through an unexpected divorce. She was a fundamentalist Christian, and her husband's sudden departure from their marriage had rocked the foundations of her world. She couldn't understand how this divorce was part of God's will for her, but she had been told all her life that doubt was evil and should be repressed. Her inability to shake the evil of doubt led to depression. She made progress only when she played with her own paradigm of reality. Instead of repressing it, I asked her to consider these questions: "Where does doubt fit in your faith? How might it help change you into a better Christian?" On reflection, she remembered Jesus' words to the Father on the cross: "Why have you forsaken me?" And she saw how it could make for better Christians: by making us humble, encouraging us to soften our inflated ideas and egos, and grounding us in our humanity. Faith was not a matter of praying to God to give us answers but rather learning to live more deeply with the ever-present uncertainty that is our life.

Accepting that we are fallible doesn't keep us from thinking that we're right: *It just keeps us from thinking that we couldn't possibly be wrong.* And that's a good thing. The ability to revise beliefs in light of new information is part of what makes having a mind worthwhile. We take stands and affirm our current position, knowing that it is one of many perspectives. And it can save us from the excesses of rigid beliefs rooted in literalism, such as the supposed evil of homosexuality and the subjugation of women.

Acknowledging our fallibility opens a window of doubt, just big enough to prevent us from using or accepting cruelty in the pursuit of our ideals. It forces us to be guided, not by our own certainties and dogmas but by the universal precept: the Golden Rule. If we are guided by charity to all, rather than our specific mythologies, we are less likely to burn our fellow beings at the stake, threaten them (as Meister Eckhart was, whose meaty soul was almost broiled as an inquisition steak), incinerate them in gas chambers and crematoriums, or commit the thousand small acts that make life harder for them, like denying health care to the poor, workplace protections to gays, and equal access to our public spaces because of private prejudices.

Religion has often taken hard lines on matters that turned out to be only of passing interest. Early Christianity barred women from wearing short hair. Heliocentrism was banned as being contrary to Scripture. Fundamentalist religion punishes sexual acts, clothing choices, even musical genres that it considers evil but that eventually may go the way of geocentrism. Adopting hard lines on marginal behaviors and ideas has time and again proved foolish, but serving others in a way that we ourselves would want to be served is always solid ground.

THE PLAYERS

Deep within play there is an ethical good grounded in the necessity for another. To play we *need* an "other"—another person, another consciousness, other skills—whether an opponent, team member, or intimate partner. Even when we play with a computer game, there is something other than ourselves engaged—the outward world and the creator of the program, the human mind that has been reified in the mechanics and aesthetics of the game. Even when we meditate, we play with sensations, images, and thoughts that constantly arise in awareness.

Knowing that we cannot play without others is the basis for a play ethic that, when deeply understood, elicits a sense of respect and appreciation for these others, our playmates and even playthings. It leads to care and gratitude, a natural valuing of this other. It also provides a hint at a virtue that has been consistent across time: that of the unity of all. Ken Wilber acknowledges this when he writes, "Are the mystics and sages insane? Because they all tell variations on the same story, don't they? The story of awakening one morning and discovering you are one with the All, in a timeless and eternal and infinite fashion. Yes, maybe they are crazy. . . . But then . . . maybe the evolutionary sequence really is from matter to body to mind to soul to spirit, each transcending and including, each with a greater depth and greater consciousness and wider embrace."[4]

The idea of unity or the oneness of all beings means that we are profoundly and inextricably related to one another. It may be as fellow travelers, forming the fellowship of the saints (as in Christianity), or it may be as part of a single timeless reality (as in Buddhism). When Jesus says that "as you do unto the least of these, you do unto me" he is destroying the fiction that there are tiers of human beings, that we can separate how we treat one person from how we treat another. Acknowledging our unity requires us to take personal responsibility for the well-being of others. This may mean showing kindness in daily life as well as pursuing social, political, economic, legal, religious, and psychological goals to achieve justice and the communal good.

Making things up acknowledges that we are all playing with different views, different experiences, and different dispositions and emotions. We make conclusions from our own observations, but we must understand that others' observations might lead to quite different conclusions—or their observations may be of things we can't see at all. Knowing this leads to mutual openness and many more options. It keeps us from getting stuck in rigidity and well-grooved thought patterns that lead nowhere. Skepticism, instead of being used to foster a particular, prejudiced, nihilistic belief of its own, can become its "best self": a check against lack of evidence, unquestioned beliefs, and overriding pronouncements. We are freed from having to understand all of reality by ourselves and from having to "win" the arguments of religion and certainty based solely on our own experiences and impressions.

Peter Berger suggests that play is an example of something he calls a "signal of transcendence," defined as a phenomenon found in the domain of our everyday reality but that also points beyond that reality.[5] Signals of transcendence are part of what Berger calls an *inductive faith*, a faith grounded in direct personal experience, unlike a deductive faith that arises from a "revealed" idea, whether from the written words in a holy book or a message given by some external authority. Inductive faith is a way of knowing based on personal, unmediated experience. Christianity took a small step toward inductive faith during the Protestant Reformation, when reformers insisted that the Bible be translated into worshippers' own languages so that it could speak directly to the reader, rather than being available only in Latin, with only priests able to interpret its meaning. But the subsequent persecution of those who deviated from the new Protestant doctrines shows just how hard breaking free is.

It may be near impossible to avoid the prior influences, prejudices, and unique perspectives that inform our experience. But starting with attention to that experience, rather than prioritizing deductive faith, is a first step. Then again hewing solely to our own experience is myopic—and frankly too great a burden on any individual. We must fully open ourselves to the experiences of others. One set of human eyes does not see the whole world. We need each other's perspectives to see the most that we can see.

THE PLAYING FIELD

We tend to think of philosophy as something in textbooks and ancient treatises. But the best philosophy is all around us, embedded in our everyday sayings and commonplaces. One of the most important is this refrain, familiar especially to golfers: "Play the ball where it lies."

This golf truism points out the supreme importance of taking life just as it is—not what we think it should be or what we feel we are entitled to. This fundamental acceptance is the basis of all happiness and is necessary to play the game of life well, sanely, saintly, and heroically. It's the principle behind Nietzsche's Will to Power, Schopenhauer's Will, Hegel's Spirit, Ramakrishna's Kali, Epictetus' God, Plato's gods, Heraclitus' Child, and Heidegger's Be-ing. It acknowledges the existence of something beyond our control, and our acceptance of the playing field that we are presented is the first step in deciding how we will play the game of life. This fundamental acceptance also is the sine qua non for real freedom, deep personal responsibility, ego-transcendence, and the Buddhist ideal of the bodhisattva.

As a spiritual path, play must grapple with the givens of life: the circumstances of our birth, the uncertainties of our progress, and the inevitability of death. Acceptance does not mean that we give up or roll over; rather it means that we grapple with the playing field that we are on and, within the reality of that field, make the best plays we can. Play as a spiritual process is the ceaseless engaging with our circumstances—not a fantasy of what might have been. Like the golfer with the ball on the rough, the best player doesn't linger on complaints and excuses but simply asks, "What's my next shot?"

Approaching life—and golf—this way leads to being disciplined, responsible, passionate, and profoundly free. The benefits of play, including its mind-altering joy, come not from winning but from playing well. When we play golf, we might take instruction on how to play, diligently following instructions, correcting mistakes, and practicing the fundamentals. We remain alert to changing conditions, a change in the direction of the wind, a downfall of rain that turns the sod sluggish. Ram Dass writes of the way aging changes our bodies and minds, but the suffering of age comes not from aging but from refusing to accept our new playing field—the body that can't move as fast, the mind that can't remember. "I've seen in interviewing old people that the minute you cling to something that was a moment ago, you suffer. You suffer when you have your face lifted to be who you wish you were then, for a little longer, because you know it's temporary."[6]

Instead of fighting change, we learn to notice it—and alter our play accordingly. Incrementally, we will eventually start to play better and better. In this way, the metaphor of play can lead us on a trajectory that begins with acceptance, takes responsibility for our moves, and ultimately ends with a life of meaning rather than escape.

The field on which we play is not just life as we know it—our circumstances, our limitations, our skills, and our fellow players. We play in *time*. This means awareness of the fleeting nature of our circumstances and feelings but also an inkling of eternity. In play, we are already in the afterlife because we move from the experience of time to the experience of timelessness, of the eternal moment. We are in *flow*, that state where time stands still or simply doesn't exist, where we are fully engaged and happy to stay right where we are.

FINAL THOUGHTS

We create, bless, and adorn reality with meaning. We do so with the paints of assumptions, prejudices, reason, and imagination all flowing into one like a watercolor landscape. We may do this like children who splash tempera on paper without much discipline or like accomplished artists who have a sense of proportion, value, and beauty. We may create our own realities with our various perspectives, each having limited value. But some rise to the surface as good, true, and beautiful by any criteria.

Karen Armstrong famously contrasted dogma-based religion with compassion-based religion.[7] This statement points the way to a new kind of given, based not on beliefs per se but on *values*. These values are exemplified by the metaphor of play: using our minds to their full creative potential; honoring others; accepting the rules of the game; and aiming to play well whatever the field looks like on any given day. These values can give us a grounding, a solid and even playing field, for our lives—and steer us away from our tendency to convert our aspirations into game and competition, with a win-all attitude that discards fair play for shady advantages.

Play is a universal good. It is the very definition of what we love to do. And the principles of play can lead us to this most universal of truths: that we should do unto others as we would want others to do unto us, and not do unto others what we would not want done unto us. The list of these unwanted things is short but powerful: the infliction of bodily pain, compulsion, neglect. The list of wanted things is just as powerful: comfort, freedom, respect, and care. And adopting the attitude of play in our spiritual life—through creativity, flanking, meditation, and all the other moves at our disposal—can bring us ever closer to them.

NOTES

1. Karen Armstrong, *A History of God: The 4,000-Year Quest of Judaism, Christianity and Islam* (New York: Ballantine, 1993).

2. Joseph Campbell, *The Hero with a Thousand Faces*, 3rd ed. (Novato, CA: New World Library, 2008).

3. It was Spariosu who asserted that "facts do not create theory; theory creates facts." Mihai Spariosu, *Dionysus Reborn: Play and the Aesthetic Dimension in Modern Philosophical and Scientific Discourse* (Ithaca, NY: Cornell University Press, 1989). In contrast to the previous view of scientific certainty, Feyerabend posited that scientific knowledge, indeed all knowledge, develops its tools in the same way that infants develop language skills, by playing games with new words and concepts until something connects and "makes sense," however tentative and non-absolute that sense may be. One plays with ideas and concepts counterinductively, with prejudice, with presumption, full of intuitive and counter-intuitive juxtapositioning with an opportunistic, ego-driven bent that is far from a "rational process." Paul Feyerabend, *Against Method: Outline of an Anarchistic Theory of Knowledge*, 3rd ed. (London: Verso, 1993).

4. Ken Wilber, *A Brief History of Everything* (Boston: Shambhala, 1996), 42.

5. Peter Berger, *A Rumor of Angels: Modern Society and the Rediscovery of the Supernatural* (New York: Doubleday, 1969).

6. Ram Dass, "Why Is It So Important to Come to Terms with Aging?" *Ram Dass* blog, November 27, 2017, https://www.ramdass.org/important-come-terms-aging/

7. Armstrong, *History of God.*

Chapter 8

Epilogue

The Final Hole

"Rule 13-1. General. The ball must be played as it lies."

—Rules and Decision, USGA

In 2012, when I first noticed difficulty swallowing where the esophagus and stomach meet, I made my own diagnosis. I felt sure it was either scleroderma, esophagitis, GERD, an esophageal ulcer, an age-related physiological change, or a rare disease called achalasia. I dismissed cancer for rather suspect reasons and felt sure, a few months later when my University of Chicago surgeon had diagnosed me with stage 4 gastroesophageal junction (GEJ) cancer and its eleven-month survival period, that the surgeon was mistaken. But the barium and the CT scan and the endoscopy ultrasound at Wisconsin told the same story.

The word *acceptance* usually means consenting to receive or undertake something offered, as in agreeing to receive a gift or take on a job opportunity. However, the disease of cancer is not an offering we freely accept. It comes without our consent. It imposes its crazy cytology and forces us to be its unwilling host as it eats through us one metastatic bite at a time. It is disruptive, chaotic, evil, and really, really scary.

When I got my diagnosis, I felt like I had entered the twilight zone. Everything seemed like a Salvador Dali painting—featureless landscapes with Quixotic figures and liquid watches dripping over the edges. This was not acceptance; this was an imposed horror on a collapsed victim struggling to stand up after being hit with a hammer on the side of the head. Hearing the diagnosis and then the confirming second opinion, I poured myself a drink of denial and followed up with a cigarette of defiance. I saw tears welling up in my wife's eyes and took another shot.

Many cancer patients are angry and strike out randomly and helplessly. They blame their physician for bringing the bad news. They boil with perceived provocation from their wives and husbands and explode over their adolescent's noncompliance. They lump medicine, Big Pharma, ACA, and their physicians together in a money-grabbing conspiracy. Or they retreat and hide under a blanket of confusion and fear. Some become so overwhelmed that they give up and give into the red-toothed voraciousness of this menace. They simply have no will to fight anymore and allow the monster to eat away, to their and its death.

But between denial and hopelessness, there is a middle way. This middle way seeks life and emphasizes all that is life-giving from the molecular to the universal level. It acknowledges that fighting is sometimes necessary but not desirable when other measures offer better benefits. Knowing that fighting ironically exacerbates conflict and problems instead of resolving them, like Brer Rabbit tackling Uncle Remus's Tar Baby, we can practice acceptance.

Acceptance seems like such a simple, even simplistic word, and it often carries a whiff of passivity. Our power-oriented culture tolerates and rewards aggressive behavior, values power and domination. Winning—as measured by wealth, prestige, and possessions—determines one's worth, far too often. Even self-improvement efforts are geared toward getting happier, stronger, smarter, and richer—to be more than we are, and hopefully more than our neighbors are. This sets up success–failure, good–bad, strong–weak, rich–poor dichotomies. It reinforces our separateness from one another, our anger and hatred for winners because they won and for losers because they lost. Those who quit, who don't fight back, are doormats, roadkill, "surrender monkeys." For fear of being seen as doormats, we are highly reactive to anything that seems dismissing, embarrassing, or disrespecting of us. We are encouraged to kick ass and take names afterward, to dominate others with trash talk and displays of one-upmanship. We will do anything but seem a weak and passive victim.

For some people, acceptance is worse than passivity; it is collaboration in maintaining a cruel status quo. Critical theorist Slavoj Zizek argues that "Buddhism is the perfect spiritual tradition to be co-opted by our self-absorbed, destructive, and consumeristic society.... Buddhism represents the perfect ideology for passive acquiescence to the world as it is"; Zizek writes that the Western take on Buddhism allow us to "fully participate in the frantic pace of the capitalist game, while sustaining the perception that you are not really in it, that you are well aware how worthless the spectacle is—what really matters to you is the peace of the inner self to which you know you can always withdraw."[1]

But acceptance in the spiritual sense is none of these things, neither passivity nor self-protection. As Buddhist teacher and writer Ethan Nichtern counters,

> mindfulness—paying direct attention to what our thoughts do in the present moment—is not at all peaceful, at least not in the 'easy' sense of the word. . . . Coming back to the moment again and again is a true revolution against habit, a rebellion against our cultural tendency to always avoid what we are feeling and experiencing. It is this chronic avoidance of ourselves (not the rigorous practice of self-awareness [that] we do on a cushion) that lies at the core of mindless consumer culture. Without having an actual practice, however, there's no way Slavoj Zizek or any of the rest of us could really see the irony of this realization.[2]

For Buddhists like Nichtern, "Practical transformation is what Buddhist practice is all about. It's also about changing the world. To practice meditation consistently is to push back hard against the tidal wave of materialism that is quite literally killing the planet."[3] Through meditation we come to perceive what we really like and what we really value. We confront our flaws and learn to love ourselves—and others just the same. Ego-transformation is the quintessential criterion for genuine spirituality. If there is no ego-transformation, if one does not see the interconnection of all things and the ethics that follows, then meditation and acceptance are indeed nothing but a "mental cocoon." As Nichtern says, "the danger is thinking that acceptance is the end of the journey."

The end of the journey provides the greatest challenge to any human being. We are faced with separation from everything we hold dear—our loved ones, our beautiful world, our joys, and our own dear self. We realize how profoundly attached we still are to all that we were—long ago—supposed to have detached from. But it is just at this moment of loss that we can see the fruits of our spiritual practice, whatever it may be. For me, Vipassana meditation let me experience, again and again, the beauty of the current moment. It allowed me to loosen my grip on the subjective ego, or "little self," and gain a sense of the larger picture. It let me profoundly understand that life is not fair, that we are infinitely small and largely unimportant in the bigger sense of reality, but that we are also integral to the ever-evolving self insofar as we understand our role as open-hearted, kind, compassionate, deeply wise human beings. Buddhist acceptance is already grounded in a death: a loss of the subjective self and a realization of one's small but important role in the evolving universe, as the bodhisattvas know. It also allows us to accept the corresponding gift that we are part of everything and everyone.

And when the day of bad news is done, we can go home to a quiet place and enter the liminal space of meditation. We acknowledge what is, then pause and allow new possibilities to emerge. Instead of a narrow and predictable reaction, this pause of awareness and acceptance permits new and even creative options that benefit everyone. We can reject the reactions that come all too easily: fighting or surrendering, winning or losing. We can reject even the trope of the patient who is determined to "kick cancer's ass." Whatever we are experiencing—a tight stomach and a clenched jaw that indicate anger and frustration; feelings of weakness and fatigue that indicate sadness—we can acknowledge and accept. If we cannot accept it, then we can accept that we cannot accept it. Each moment of acknowledging our reality is a step toward wisdom.[4]

We can become open to cancer as a teacher. But to do this we have to see that our emotions are passing phenomena that have a very brief half-life. They are our emotions, but they quickly fade. And they are not really *us*. We are not a shame-person, a guilt-person, a depression-person. We are simply the river that these grains of sand and boulders run through, the being that breathes these emotions in and out as they arise. Just notice them. They are not you; they are mere phenomena that have come to visit. Like houseguests who have overstayed their welcome, they must be shown the door when they have clung too long to our hospitality.

It can be easy to want to resist feeling these things when they turn up in your life; after all, they *hurt*, and who wants that? But sometimes resisting them, or denying them, or expending your energy wishing them away can come at a cost of its own. Feeling bad about feeling bad can bring a second order of pain into your life, a whole new level of suffering that's layered on top of the original hurt. Denial is a fight, but there are other options. We can walk *toward* the pain rather than trying to run *away* from it. Welcome it. Get to know it. See what it's all about. *Play* with it.

In my field of psychology there is an approach called acceptance and commitment therapy. Its core is that we should not try to reduce symptoms but rather radically accept that suffering and even destructive habits of mind are normal. The irony is that when we lay down our arms and stop fighting this truth, our symptoms fade on their own.[5] It's a bit like the Gestalt therapy idea called "the paradoxical theory of change" that posits that we change when we accept who we are rather than trying to change who we are.[6]

Essentially, all of these concepts are about sitting with what *is*, good or bad. So if there's pain, then it means staying with it for a moment. And if there's joy, then it's about really embracing that, too. If you stop resisting pain and just allow it to sit next to you—if you just let what is *be*—then you've already changed your relationship to it. And you've let it change its relationship to you. Rather than trying to control the pain and build ever bigger dams inside to keep it all at bay, if you just accept it, the paradoxical theory of change suggests that it may well just wash in and through and out of you again. And then other things have a chance to flow in in its place. The poet Rumi was already onto this in the thirteenth century in his poem "The Guest House."[7] And we are still learning it today.

One gift from cancer is the advanced notice that affords the opportunity to reassess and reprioritize. It counsels bypassing the unnecessary and stopping to notice what matters. There is a reconsideration, a reprioritizing, a recalibration, and a revaluation of one's life. When I received my diagnosis, my first instinct was rage. But even then, in those first moments, I heard a voice in the back of my head saying, "How do you want to play this?"

Some make wills for the first time, draw up bucket lists, contact long-lost friends, write memoirs, visit their ancestral homeland, and tell loved ones, maybe for the first time ever, that they are loved. There is an urgency to do so. The saying "life's too short" makes unquestionable sense as we thank God for the time to wedge everything in.

But cancer can just as easily move us to accept that life really *is* too short. We will never check off our bucket list, repair every mistake, and perfect every creation. And that's okay. Letting things go unfinished is normal. Falling short is normal. Not reaching our full potential is normal. These failures are human, a nod to our mortality, not tragedies.

Away from city lights, we can look into the night and see an infinite sky. This immensity gently reminds us of our smallness, just as it did when we were children. The roar of this universe, which has resounded long before us and will echo long after we are dust, dissolves any self-important protests into an awe-filled silence. To the cosmic eye that gazes back to the Big Bang and possibly before, humankind is a mere wink and maybe a nod. Earth has endured at least five extinctions to life with the promise of another, whether from cosmic intrusion or human stupidity. Do we collectively, much less individually, really make any difference in the grandest of schemes? What we think is important is just a sigh in the breathing of time.

We all have our beliefs and theories about our life's value and purpose or lack thereof. But when we get down to it, proof will never be in our grasp. Joseph Campbell wrote that we make meaning with self-sustaining myths about reality. Myths change and become more complex as we evolve from prehistoric cave painters to technological creators of all things great and small. Campbell believed that all myth-making arises from the innate ability of humans to play. We make things up, creating realities with imaginations that hopefully make our world better, although the materialization of that hope is always hanging in the balance.

My playing with the nature of the world has led me to some as-ifs of my own. Time is fashioned, drawn, and shot by God, but time is not eternal. Christian theologians cite their champion, St. Augustine, who said that everything, including our universe and time, began with God. Nothing existed before. Einstein's general theory of relativity has led modern cosmologists to Augustine's same conclusion about our finite origin. Stephen Hawking and Roger Penrose proved in the 1960s that time and other quantities cannot extend backward indefinitely. They wrote that as cosmic history plays back in time, galaxies come together and squeeze into a single infinitesimal point, a singularity. Space-time compresses as if into a black hole beyond which our cosmic ancestry cannot extend and from which time and our universe boomed into being.

Perhaps, the image of an arrow is too linear. Perhaps, time is more like a boomerang that forever circles back. Either way, two things are certain: The arrow of time kills all of us, and a life that transcends ego and cares and loves all creation is a good and meaningful life regardless of what comes after. We may not have tomorrow. All of us, one day, will not have tomorrow. But I play whatever days I have left with the beautiful image of eternity in my sights.

NOTES

1. Ethan Nichtern, "Radical Buddhism and the Paradox of Acceptance," *HuffPost*, August 29, 2010, https://www.huffpost.com/entry/radical-buddhism_b_671972. See also Slavoj Žižek, "From Western Marxism to Western Buddhism," *Cabinet* magazine 2 (Spring 2001), http://www.cabinetmagazine.org/issues/2/western.php.

2. Nichtern, "Radical Buddhism and the Paradox of Acceptance."

3. Nichtern, "Radical Buddhism and the Paradox of Acceptance."

4. A beautiful story of such acceptance can be found in Bobbi Emel, "How Resisting Causes More Pain: Accept and Help Yourself Heal," https://tinybuddha.com/blog/when-resisting-causes-more-pain-accept-and-help-yourself-heal/.

5. Russell Harris, "Embracing Your Demons: An Overview of Acceptance and Commitment Therapy," *Psychotherapy in Australia* 12, no. 4 (August 2006): 2–8.

6. Arnold Beisser, "The Paradoxical Theory of Change," http://www.gestalt.org/arnie.htm.

7. Jellaludin Rumi, "The Guest House," in *The Illustrated Rumi*, trans. Coleman Barks (New York: Broadway Books, 1997).

Appendix
How to Meditate

So, after all this talk, what if you want to play with the meditative experience? Let's look at what meditation in day-to-day life looks like.

Gary tries not to think about it. When he does, the part of him that says "Enjoy the warm bed" usually wins. So when the alarm goes off at 4:35 a.m., he reaches over, flips it off, and forces two feet to the ground. In a mist of sleepiness, he wobbles to the bathroom, then he pets and feeds Tazu, his kitty.

This routine transports him to the shower, leads him to brush his teeth, and gets him dressed. As a college athlete, he learned that routine is an express train, without the stops of thought and choice. Gary grudgingly admits that Nike's right: "Just do it!"

This morning is no different. Gary puts a maroon wrap around his shoulders and begins. He sits on a pillow, back straight, legs crossed, hands in lap, eyes closed, and lifts his lips into a faint smile. He lets his breath fill his awareness. He feels his stomach, chest, and shoulders waltz to the in-and-out rhythm of the air through his nostrils. His jaw and thighs ease while his breath slow dances to the soft beat of his heart. This awareness dances over his body. An ear itch, an arm twitch, an ankle pain, a glow in his loins come and go along with a thousand other sensations. His hand moves toward an itch and drops back into his lap along with that inner judge who criticizes his less-than-perfect practice. Gently, he returns his concentration to the natural cycle of his breath.

He sits on a knoll in his mind and watches a schoolyard of rambunctious images, thoughts, and sensations—"stuff" he calls this—inviting him to play. Their allure is compelling and soon Gary is debating between eggs or oatmeal for breakfast. His mind rolls out last Saturday's bike ride with his granddaughter and tosses up what she will grow into being. Next his mind plays dodgeball with his cigarette addiction, teeter-totters on whether to wash windows or cut grass, and arm-wrestles with his editor over an ending to a short story. He wants to scratch the accompanying itches. His mind is having a typically rowdy day.

Gary smiles that this kids' stuff got him again. Back on his mind's knoll, he floats in his breath's calm awareness that trickles over the "stuff" like raindrops down a window pane.

Usually, this is about as far as it goes: a playground of stuff competing with calm awareness, indifferent to competition. But this morning is turning out differently. Gradually, his mind's sundry play melts away. Gary's awareness falls like a soft summer shower. Stuff collects in runnels and whirlpools down a drain. There is only a kind of wet awareness on a featureless, motionless playground. All dissolves in and as this wetness, including time, space, Gary, and his breathing. On an ocean horizon in a starless winter's night, wetness itself evaporates like a raindrop on a sunny summer day.

Tazu crawls under the wrap, purrs in his lap, and joins this awareness. Gary feels a tear fall down his cheek, a peaceful raindrop of this–other worldly joy. Maybe this is why he just does it. But this doesn't quite do it. There is no explanation. It's a raindrop without a why.

An egg timer signals the passing hour. He drops his wrap, rolls his neck, and lets his heart whisper: "May all being be filled with lovingkindness, may all be well, may all be peaceful and at ease, may all be happy." With this, Gary walks into his day. He knows that he will begin again tomorrow. And the next day, and the next. Without thinking about it.

Jeff, an amateur race car driver with a cursory knowledge of meditation, views both as a challenge which seems intrinsic to all play. These playful challenges require goals, concentration, endurance, and skill. Jeff says, "No way someone just hops into a race car, steps on the gas, and wins a race." He knows too that a person can't just sit down, close their eyes, and meditate successfully. Winning a race or realizing enlightenment helps frame the goal and direction of these activities. The goal is like a mountain in the distance, but the focused discipline and necessary skill to drive down the road toward that mountain are what gets you there.

Race driving and meditation aren't exactly fun, but they are satisfying and meaningful. Both have hazards and surprises that challenge here-and-now attention and call for expert adjustments. To be able to maintain skillful focus with adroit responses brings a joy beyond fun. This joy is not only a "feel good" for having accomplished something that we hadn't done before, but a joy that arises from allowing something deeper, not previously experienced, to arise in appreciative surprise.

Jeff, with the skill that comes with thirty years of racing, emphasized "trusting the race," which means trusting the playful process without thinking about it. "If you start thinking and worrying, you crash and lose. Just drive, baby, drive!" The same is true of skillful meditation and perhaps of play in general. Concentrate, don't think. Respond, don't react. Move on, don't balk. Trust the process, don't fight it. Fearlessly engage the process with open receptivity and calm awareness. Let the openings come naturally. With detached composure, move into the gaps, whether between cars or the debris of awareness.

Mary, a writer, considers her meditation to be a play-like adventure. "Have a general direction and go with it. This is what play is all about," she says. She referred to a trip she took with her husband. They flipped coins to determine a direction for their one-week vacation. Driving south, they stopped at parks to fish, picnic, and hike. They visited museums and historical landmarks. They ate at funky restaurants, talked to the locals, slept under the stars or in roadside motels when it rained. Nothing was planned, everything was done spontaneously. One night in St. Louis, after touring the Arch, they ventured into a nightclub where the Drifters were performing and ended up talking and laughing with the group over a predawn breakfast.

Mary says that meditation is like this, an unplanned adventure. "You don't know where it'll take you. It's an adventure to unknown territory where few people go. Once you have the goal and follow the directions, you let go of expectations. Often meditation is just plain dull, but sometimes it's radiant. Either way, I just try to roll with it and take what comes."

Mary shyly mentions how the calm, sustained, inner silence of meditation is a mind–body adventure. The mind keeps generating thought after thought and sensations ceaselessly come and go throughout her body. She read from her journal. "It's 5 a.m. as I gaze from the deck of our cruise ship in the Inside Passage of Southeast Alaska. Eagles fly overhead, salmon jump in the steel blue water, white caps slosh up and down and over another, and a gray rain cloud pours over a mountain's lip in a nearby fjord. Everything moves in the silence. A whale breaches, my jaw drops. I, the only witness, no one else. Then it's all back. Eagles, salmon, white caps, rain clouds move in an endless silence."

For Mary, meditation is like noticing the constantly changing movement of eagles and rain clouds. As the play of meditative awareness and nonreactive calmness deepen, occasionally a brief experience of a "peaceful joy beyond bliss" spontaneously arises. She said that this pure joy and awe were like her experience of the breaching whale, but much deeper.

Then she says something surprising. She notes that she began to look forward to the "breaching whale of bliss." Her teacher recommended that she let go and move on with the calm awareness, that this whale of bliss was like the eagles and rain clouds, just one more event in the ceaseless play of phenomenon. She recognized that desiring this bliss was delaying her adventure into even deeper "inside passages."

Mary continues her meditative adventure. She laughs that she no longer talks about her "latest and greatest" meditative experiences. This is a little like talking about your book before it's finished. You're out of the mode of doing it and into the mode of describing it. She just hopes other people would take the journey, because "there's nothing like it."

Kim, a former college basketball player, veteran meditator, and now a mother of two, views everything she does as play. Sacrifice and gain, fun and hard work, focus, repeating the details, making others as important as yourself. Sports and mothering and meditation all require concentration, putting your whole mind-body self into it. They are all simultaneously active and passive, initiating and receptive, at times taking the game (pushing the game energy and intensity) to your opponent and at others letting the game come to you (taking advantage of what other team gives you), depending on the flow of the game. Mental state is both completely in touch with the surrounding goings-on and strangely detached from it.

Kim says, "I commit myself, perfect the skills, and keep doing it until it's automatic. It's easier for athletes to view everything as play. Whether it's sports, relationships, or meditation, it all play for me. I'd go nutso if it was just work."

"Playing does something else: it takes me out of myself," she says. "It's easy to see this in team sports because it's not about you, it's about the team. There's definitely an 'I' in 'child,' but none in 'team' and especially none in 'mother.' But the 'I' in meditation is the most fun. There's the real challenge. It keeps popping up, wanting this, hating that, much worse than a selfish teammate or a bratty child—because it's a constant and demanding whining inside you. Going beyond the ego is truly a game worth playing and as far as I know it's only done well through wise compassion and meditation. Can you think of a more extreme and challenging game than transcending the ego? Can you imagine anything more meaningful than emptying your heart and mind for the good of others? What's really cool is that losing in this game is winning it."

She understands all these activities as skilled and disciplined play that occasionally evoke ecstasy. "Of course there are moments of spontaneous joy, that come out of nowhere. But the ones that indelibly touch you come from conscious and dedicated practice." Kim describes the long, frustrating, and seemingly unproductive hours she puts into these activities. Perfecting these crafts often requires a daily recommitment. "Routine helps, reading helps, supportive people help. But just doing it without seeing progress or knowing the outcome, that's the difficult part, especially with parenting." She points out that play usually has a mix of uncertainty, risk, and possibility. "You can read about it, make preparations, learn tips for traveling, but the journey is always uncertain." If you have an adventurous heart, this uncertainty makes the play even more meaningful.

And what about you? What would your meditation in day-to-day life look like? Although the meditative experience can never be precisely defined, there are some general categories of meditation that you can use to begin with.

ATTENTIONAL FOCUS MEDITATION

Attentional focus meditation is a meditation in which the meditator concentrates on either one object (focused attention, or FA) or all phenomena (open-monitoring, or OM).

Examples of FA would be attention to breath, sensation, visualization (an image like Gary's knoll, or some image of loving-kindness or compassion), an external stimulus (like a sound or candle), a mantra (a word, phrase, or sound), a religious object or idea (cross, skull, theological mystery), a sound (chanting), energy in body (chakras), or even walking.

OM would be a nonreactive, nonjudgmental monitoring of the content of all experience from moment to moment. You focus on what is happening around you, what you're feeling, what thoughts are passing through your mind, without wanting to change them or even embrace them. You simply observe them as they are.

There are many variations of FA. Evidence from neuroimaging studies suggests that the categories of meditation, defined by how they direct attention, appear to generate different brainwave patterns. Evidence also suggests that, even within one category of meditation such as FA, using different focus objects may generate different brainwave patterns. Other variations include "movement in stillness," where one observes a wild river of moment-to-moment phenomena while engaged in sitting meditation. Or one can have "stillness in movement" where one moves the body (e.g., in Qigong exercises or simply everyday activity) with calm FA.

How to Start with Focused Attention

To actually practice FA meditation, you will be focusing attention on an object, allowing your focus to gradually become calmer and more concentrated. In principle, any object will do—a sound, a visual image such as a candle flame, or a physical sensation. In the tantric Buddhism of Tibet and elsewhere, meditators visualize complex images of Buddha forms and recite sacred sounds or mantras. But the most common and basic object of concentrative meditation is to focus on the naturally calming physical process of the breath.

Starting the practice can be as simply as sitting cross-legged on your bed and closing your eyes. It can be as complex as donning special clothing, making precise adjustments to your environment, having a special chair or room, and so on.

Once settled, you begin. Here is a common version of the practice:

- In the first stage of the practice you follow the breath as it enters and leaves the body and count after the out-breath. After the first breath you count "two" and so on up to ten and then start again from one.
- In the second stage the count comes before the in-breath.
- In the third stage you stop counting and attend to the sensations of the breath entering and leaving the body.
- In the fourth stage you focus your attention on the tip of your nose where the breath first comes into contact with the skin.

GENERATIVE MEDITATION

Generative meditation is intended to produce (generate) attitudes of compassion and ego-transformation. An example of a generative practice is the loving-kindness meditation known as "metta bhavana." "Metta" means (non-romantic) love and is referred to in the Buddhist scriptures this way: "As a mother would risk her life to protect her child, her only child, even so should one cultivate a limitless heart with regard to all beings. With goodwill for the entire cosmos cultivate a limitless heart."[1] Metta bhavana helps the person meditating to develop an attitude of loving-kindness using memory, imagination, and awareness of bodily sensations.

Other generative practices in Buddhism include *tonglen*, the Tibetan practice of breathing in the suffering of others and breathing out a purifying white light.

How to Start with Generative Meditation

To practice metta, you situate yourself as in attentional focus, ideally somewhere quiet. The practice then proceeds this way:

- In the first stage you feel metta for yourself with the help of an image like golden light or phrases such as "May I be well and happy, may I progress."
- In the second stage you think of a good friend and, using an image, a phrase, or simply the feeling of love, you develop metta toward them.
- In the third stage metta is directed toward someone you do not particularly like or dislike, someone you feel fairly neutral about.
- In the fourth stage it is directed towards someone you actually dislike.
- In the last stage, you feel metta for all four people at once—yourself, the friend, the neutral person, and the enemy. Then you extend the feeling of love from your heart to everyone in the world, to all beings everywhere.

RECEPTIVE MEDITATION

In the mindfulness of breathing or the metta bhavana meditation practice, a balance needs to be struck between consciously guiding attention and being receptive to whatever experience is arising. This attitude of open receptive attention is the emphasis of the receptive type of meditation practice.

Sometimes such practices are simply concerned with being mindful. In the *zazen* or "just sitting" practice from the Japanese Zen tradition, one sits calmly, aware of what is happening in one's experience without judging, fantasizing, or trying to change things—very similar to an OM technique. A similar practice in Tibetan tradition is *dzogchen*. In both cases, the meditator sits with their eyes open (rather than closed, as is more usual). Zazen and dzogchen practices gain depth from the underlying belief in the significance of being in the present moment. Receptive meditation is very similar to open monitoring but with more of a balance between monitoring and focusing.

REFLECTIVE MEDITATION

Reflective meditation is the mirror image of receptive meditation. It is very similar to FA but with more of a balance between focusing and monitoring. The meditator turns their attention repeatedly to a theme but is open to whatever arises from the experience. Reflective practices in Buddhism include meditations on impermanence and interconnectedness as well as faith-enhancing practices such as meditation on the qualities of the Buddha.

OTHER TYPES OF MEDITATION

Secular meditation is not a different practice in itself; it is the use of any meditative practices for the purpose of promoting physical and mental health. Often referred to as "mindfulness," secular meditation has an emphasis on what *works*. Science has confirmed the physical and mental benefits of meditation. What is lacking in secular meditation is the spiritual element that is part and parcel of traditional practices.

Sometimes secular meditation employs consciousness-altering substances as a means to practice meditation and gain enlightenment. This element has a long history in both secular and spiritual meditation traditions.[2]

Religious meditation seeks mystical and often ultimate reality through unity and identification with the Ultimate itself. It is distinguished by the inclusion of a Divine Playmate and seeks to know God. Traditional prayer is a type of religious meditation. There are thousands of variations of religious meditation.

ONE MORE MEDITATOR'S STORY

When I told the stories of Gary, Jeff, Mary, and Kim, I forgot one other story—Mark's. Yes, mine.

When I started practicing Vipassana meditation years ago, I never dreamed that I would end up in retreats, sitting motionless for twelve hours a day, with only two vegetarian meals a day, walking in subzero weather for exercise, and giving up all outside means of entertainment, including television (yawn), cell phones (whatever), and books (oh no!). But I like adventures of a different sort. As an former athlete and nature lover, I understand the idea of "no pain–no gain" boot camps, challenging treks, and climbing mountains because they're there, where discipline and discomfort are part of a larger goal of discovery and achievement. And as a therapist who daily works with psychological processes, I'm fascinated by what I call the "inside passage" opened up by meditation, where the fascinating workings of the mind-body are available for observation. I'm always amazed at how unaware many people are of what goes on in their bodies and between their ears.

Of course, the skeptic in me thoroughly investigated meditation before I started in earnest in 2007. The research overwhelmingly supports the use of daily meditation to lower stress and reduce reactivity to negative events. Meditation retrains the brain for resiliency and optimism and helps develop clarity and calm when facing difficulties, even serious illness and death. With psychotherapy, it is used to treat physical pain, post-traumatic stress, hypochondriasis, borderline personality disorder, addictions, and even some forms of psychosis. There are indications that it also facilitates physical healing. Meditation seems especially compatible with cognitive behavioral therapy because of their common attention to altering thought processes that produce unnecessary suffering. Obviously, simply reading about all this wasn't going to help me, and recommending that my patients use it without my also doing so was disingenuous.

I investigated different kinds of meditation. I had learned Transcendental Meditation when I was in graduate school but with little success, in part because it lacked a strong ethical component. Somehow, smoking grass, getting drunk, partying, and living a less than moral life with little concern for kind compassion but still meditating with my mantra seemed incongruous. Other forms of meditation paid attention to the in-out breath around the nostrils (*anapanna*) or attention to all phenomena (thoughts, emotions, images), as in Zen meditation (*zazen*). But Vipassana meditation focused specifically on the body's vast array of sensations, and it was in Vipassana that I found the fruit of ego-transformation most abundantly supplied.

What I found through my journey is that meditation does not remove pain and pleasure; rather it removes suffering and addiction. It does not undermine our close attachments to others; rather it clears away the delusion that we are separate from others. It does not make us neutral in our reactions; rather it creates a space between sensations and reactions in which I can respond in the most compassionate manner possible. It becomes clear that awareness plus equanimity provides the foundation for responding calmly to any stimuli both within the body-mind and outside in the environment. This simple technique interrupts knee-jerk reactions and offers a ground to make better and hopefully more healthy and loving responses.

This meditation promises no instant results, no sudden enlightenment, no radical change of heart. Rather, it insists on sustained, incremental progress for the practitioner's development. It cautions against any "feel good" outcomes, but rather regards "good" and "bad" meditative experiences as the same. There is no proselytizing. Emphasis is placed on self-verification: "Try this, follow the instructions (and they are exacting!), and see for yourself." No fee is charged for a retreat, the organization I was involved in never asks for donations, and there is no pressure to join volunteer committees. If a donation is given, it is never for oneself and only for the next person who wishes to learn the technique. Feeding and helping students at retreats or helping with the maintenance of centers are common volunteer activities.

Someone asked about the spiritual benefits of this meditation. Because this form of Vipassana meditation is presented as a psychological technique that is helpful to everyone, mention of religion and spirituality is absent.

Nevertheless, there is an underlying epistemology or "way of knowing" that permeates this teaching, which clearly follows Buddhist psychology and spirituality. First, there is emphasis on the three perennial aspects for all spiritual disciplines: ethics, philosophy, and practice, each interrelated and necessary for transformative effect. Second, the technique follows the four noble truths of Buddhism: the fact of suffering, the origin of suffering, the cessation of suffering, and path that leads to the cessation of suffering. Third, there is silence when it comes to a supernatural force or deity. God is neither affirmed nor denied. The ultimate goal of the technique, when practiced ethically and compassionately, is enlightenment or liberation—a release from the grip of endless craving and aversion. Success is a matter of deep, inner personal responsibility and not due to some outside magic, grace, or intervention from a supernatural source. Paradoxically, the goal of enlightenment is realized when one releases the goal of enlightenment. Enlightenment arises when one lives detached from egoic desire and fully engaged in wise, kind, and compassionate action for the well-being of others.

On several occasions while meditating, I have had brief and surprising moments of deep bliss. They came out of nowhere (sometimes when I was most struggling to focus) and lasted no more than ten minutes. I simply realized "This is it." There was no more Mark in that experience. I wasn't there. Only this "beyond bliss" disembodied, absorbing experience remained.

Pleasure, like pain, pertains to the nervous system. Bliss belongs to an entirely different order of existence. It is not a feeling or sensation but rather that condition which prevails when all feelings and sensations as well as thoughts have been eclipsed by the realization of sheer Being. True, ecstatic bliss is apt to register in the body, but the body, as we ordinarily experience it, is not its source. In the ecstatic condition of identity with Being, the body stands revealed as the universe itself. The physical frame is found to be not solid after all but a vast ocean of energy in which all bodies are interconnected. Thus, bliss cannot be said to have any location or any cause.

Clearly, my neuro-bio-chemical apparatus was firing on all cylinders, but I don't think it wise to reduce the experience merely to a scientific explanation. Nor do I think I am unusual or enlightened. The meditation literature views these "beyond bliss" moments as common, about a stage 4 on a scale of 50 in terms of enlightenment realization. Many of the next steps suggest relinquishing attachment to these super-blissful states, viewing them as just one more event in the ceaseless play of phenomena. Still, these are experiences that I will never forget.

For those interested in the type of meditation that I practice, I recommend U Silananda's "Meditation Instructions," a description of the Vipassana meditation practice.[3]

THE SCIENCE OF MEDITATION

The authenticity of the meditative experience is rooted in the meditator's own ego-transformation and the devotion of generations of meditators. But it's important to note that the benefits of meditation have now been studied extensively by scientists, and the results of those studies have validated the meditators' subjective experiences. This sections of the appendix turns from the spiritual heights to see how meditation works in the everyday world.

For example, a rich mine of research on pain has been tapped in recent years.[4] The total annual incremental cost of health care due to pain ranges from $560 billion to $635 billion (in 2010 dollars) in the United States, which combines the medical costs of pain care and the economic costs related to disability days and lost wages and productivity. In 2011, at least 100 million adult Americans reported common chronic pain conditions, and sales of OPR (opioid pain relievers) quadrupled between 1999 and 2010. Though many of us would side with Oscar Wilde when he says, "God spare me physical pain, and I'll take care of moral pain myself," it's worth noting that high percentages of those who suffer chronic pain report depression, low energy, and the inability to sleep well.

The question becomes how best to address chronic pain. Opioids have wreaked havoc on American society, destroying lives and creating pockets of despair in the worst-hit areas, like West Virginia. *USA Today* reported that

> Congressional investigators found that, between 2007 and 2012, distributors sent more than 780 million hydrocodone and oxycodone into West Virginia, which roughly equals 433 pills for every man, woman and child in the state, congressional investigators say. During that time, 1,728 West Virginians fatally overdosed on those two drugs.
>
> Investigators discovered that a single pharmacy in Mount Gay-Shamrock, population 1,779, received more than 16.5 million hydrocodone and oxycodone pills between 2006 and 2016. In nearby Williamson, population 2,900, distributors sent almost 21 million opioids to two pharmacies during that same period.[5]

Opioids offer an understandably compelling path of avoidance for pain sufferers. Meditation's entire structure, in contrast, is attending to what is, what you are experiencing *right now*. It would seem a poor alternative for those trying to escape the agony of chronic pain. But as Stanford lecturer Kelly McGonigal notes, it is an extremely effective approach to pain management. She discovered this subjectively herself when she injured her ankle, days before giving a lecture on how meditators experience pain:

> When I collapsed to the ground after banging my ankle on a hardwood meditation bench, I knew this was an opportunity for a scientific experiment. I had

spent the last few days preparing a talk on the neuroscience of meditation. More specifically, how meditators process pain differently than non-meditators.

The biggest difference? Meditators pay more attention to the direct sensation of pain. In laboratory studies that deliver painful stimulation, meditators' brains show more activity in areas associated with sensory processing (think: ankle throbbing!).

Non-meditators, on the other hand, showing more activity in areas associated with evaluation and language. It's the inner dialogue of "Holy $!%@ that hurts! I'm such a klutz! This stinks! When is it going to stop?"

Interestingly, the more a meditator's brain focuses on the pain experience, and the less [on] the evaluation system, the higher their pain tolerance. It's what we hear all the time from our wisest meditation teachers: Focus on the sensations, drop the story. It's the story that turns pain into suffering.[6]

Put another way, bodily discomfort has three components:

1. The unpleasant physical sensation itself (pain, aching muscles, fatigue)
2. Our emotional reaction to that discomfort (anger, frustration, fear)
3. The thoughts that are triggered by the discomfort ("This pain will never go away," "I'll never be happy again," "I've ruined my partner's life")

Note that two of the three components that make up our experience of bodily discomfort are mental in origin! They are what Rick Heller calls the "aversion response,"[7] and they can make our physical suffering worse because mental reactions are felt in the body.

Buddhists do not believe that pain is illusory, except in the sense that all transient things are. Nonetheless, the effects of meditation on pain give powerful witness to the belief that suffering (*dukkha*) is a matter of attitude rather than just biology. McGonigal's research on attending to the pain as a phenomenon rather than a story is supplemented by Melinda Beck's reporting on flanking techniques like guided imagery, which concentrate not on the pain itself but on a distracting third option.[8] What both reports share is the importance of abandoning the "story" of pain. Beck writes, "When [research subjects] 're-evaluated' their pain emotionally—'Yes, my back hurts, but I won't let that stop me'—they had more activity in the deep brain structures that process emotion. Either way, they were able to ease their own pain significantly." Beck cites Robert Coghill, a neuroscientist at Wake Forest Baptist Medical Center:

> "We are all walking around carrying the baggage [either toolboxes full of skills or full of burdensome lead weight] both good and bad, from our past experience and we use that information to make projections about what we expect to happen in the future," says Robert Coghill. . . . Dr. Coghill gives a personal

example: "I'm periodically trying to get into shape—I go to the gym and work out way too much and my muscles are really sore, but I interpret that as a positive. I'm thinking, 'I've really worked hard.'" A person with fibromyalgia might be getting similar pain signals, he says, but experience them very differently, particularly if she fears she will never get better.[9]

Fears and attitudes are powerful contributors to suffering, and Beck notes that those who adopted meditation felt freed from some of that. As researcher Fadel Zeidan put it, "Our subjects really looked at pain differently after meditating. Some said, 'I didn't need to say ouch.'" Zeidan reported a "40 percent reduction in pain intensity and a 57 percent reduction in pain unpleasantness" among his subjects.[10] When a soldier who has been shot drags a friend to safety, or an injured soccer player plays through the pain, we see the power of a compelling alternative narrative.

The way that meditation can lead to ego-transformation was illuminated by an unlikely source: a study of patients with traumatic brain injury to their right parietal lobe.[11] The researcher, Brick Johnstone, found that subjects with the greatest damage to this area reported greater feelings of spirituality—such as how close they felt to a higher power and if they felt their lives were part of a divine plan.

The kicker: The right side of the brain is associated with self-orientation, whereas the left side is associated with how individuals relate to others. "Neuropsychology researchers consistently have shown that impairment on the right side of the brain decreases one's focus on the self," Johnstone said. "Since our research shows that people with this impairment are more spiritual, this suggests spiritual experiences are associated with a decreased focus on the self. This is consistent with many religious texts that suggest people should concentrate on the well-being of others rather than on themselves."

Although Johnstone studied people with brain injury, previous studies of Buddhist meditators and Franciscan nuns with normal brain function have shown that people can learn to minimize the functioning of the right side of their brains to increase their spiritual connections during meditation and prayer. It is clear that science and religion—objective measurement and subjective experience—agree: Meditation is a powerful and positive practice.

NOTES

1. Metta sutta, https://www.accesstoinsight.org/tipitaka/kn/snp/snp.1.08.than.html.

2. Robert S. De Ropp, *The Master Game: Pathways to Higher Consciousness beyond the Drug Experience* (New York: Delacorte Press, 1968); *The Master Game:*

Pathways to Higher Consciousness (New York: Dell, 1989); *Drugs and the Mind*, new rev. ed. (New York: Delacorte Press, 1976).

3. U Silananda, "Meditation Instructions," http://www.mahabodhi.org/mla/note/meditation%20instructions,%20Vipassana%20&%20Metta.pdf. Originally published at http://www.tbsa.org/meditationinstrucctions.htm, April 24, 2006.

4. The statistics that follow come from the Institute of Medicine Report from the Committee on Advancing Pain Research, Care, and Education, *Relieving Pain in America, A Blueprint for Transforming Prevention, Care, Education and Research* (National Academies Press, 2011).

5. Michael Collins, "Opioid Distributor Apologizes for Shipping Large Volumes of Painkillers to West Virginia," *USA Today*, May 8, 2018.

6. Kelly McGonigal, "How Meditation Changes Pain, Relieves Depression: The More You Focus on Pain, the Higher Your Pain Tolerance," *Psychology Today*, September 25, 2011. See also McGonigal, "The Science of Willpower," Stanford University's Continuing Education program, http://kellymcgonigal.com/online-courses/.

7. Rick Heller, "Buddhism's Pain Relief," *Lion's Roar* blog, September 13, 2010, https://www.lionsroar.com/buddhisms-pain-relief/.

8. Melinda Beck, "Rewiring the Brain to Ease Pain Brain Scans Fuel Efforts to Teach Patients How to Short-Circuit Hurtful Signals," *WSJ Health Journal*, November 15, 2011.

9. Beck, "Rewiring the Brain."

10. "Demystifying Meditation: Brain Imaging Illustrates How Meditation Reduces Pain," *Science Daily*, April 6, 2011, https://www.sciencedaily.com/releases/2011/04/110405174835.htm.

11. Brick Johnstone and Daniel Cohen, *Neuroscience, Selflessness, and Spiritual Experience: Explaining the Science of Transcendence* (London: Academic Press, 2019).

Select Bibliography

Alexander, F. 1958. "A Contribution to the Theory of Play." *Psychoanalytic Quarterly* 27: 186–192.
App, U. 1994. *Master Yunmen: From the Record of the Ch'an Teacher: Gate of the Clouds.* New York: Kodansha International Press.
Armstrong, K. 1993. *The History of God.* New York: Ballantine.
———. 2000. *The Battle for God.* New York: Knopf.
———. 2008. "My Wish: The Charter for Compassion." TED Talk. www.ted.com.
Aron, C. 1999. *Working at Play.* Oxford: Oxford University Press.
Backman, Maurie. 2017. "Here's a New Reason to Work Fewer Hours." *The Motley Fool*, June 14.
Barron, Carrie. 2013. "Creativity and the Liminal Space." *Psychology Today*, June 4.
Bateson, G. 1955. "A Theory of Play and Fantasy." *Psychiatric Research Reports* 2: 40–51.
Beck, Melinda. 2011. "Rewiring the Brain to Ease Pain Brain Scans Fuel Efforts to Teach Patients How to Short-Circuit Hurtful Signals." *WSJ Health Journal*, November 15.
Berger, Peter. 1961. *The Precarious Vision.* Garden City, NJ: Doubleday.
———. 1990. *A Rumor of Angels.* New York: Anchor-Doubleday.
Berne, E. 1964. *Games People Play.* New York: Grove.
Beyer, Stephan, ed. and trans. 1974. *The Buddhist Experience: Sources and Interpretations.* Belmont, CA: Wadsworth.
Brown, Stuart, and Christopher Vaughn. 2009. *Play: How It Shapes the Brain, Opens the Imagination, and Invigorates the Soul.* New York: Avery.
Buber, M. 2002/1947. *Between Man and Man.* Trans. Ronald Gregor-Smith. New York: Routledge Classics.
Buxbaum, Y. 2005. *The Light and Fire of the Baal Shem Tov.* New York: Continuum.
Callois, R. 1961. *Man, Play, and Games.* New York: Schocken.
Campbell, Joseph. 1959. *Masks of God: Primitive Mythology.* New York: Viking.

———. 2008. *The Hero with a Thousand Faces*. 3rd ed. Novato, CA: New World Library.

Caputo, John D. 1977. *The Mystical Element in Heidegger's Thought*. Athens, OH: Ohio University Press.

Chesterton, G. K. 1908. "On Running after One's Hat." In *All Things Considered*. New York: J. Lane, 23–26.

Claparede, E. 1911. *Experimental Pedagogy and the Psychology of the Child*. London: Edward Arnold.

Committee on Advancing Pain Research, Care, and Education. 2011. *Institute of Medicine Report: Relieving Pain in America, A Blueprint for Transforming Prevention, Care, Education and Research*. National Academies Press.

Cooley, C. 1922. *Human Nature and the Social Order*. New York: Scribner.

Csikszentmihalyi, M. 1990. *Flow*. New York: Harper and Row.

———. 1975. *Beyond Boredom and Anxiety*. San Francisco: Jossey-Bass.

———. 1993. *The Evolving Self*. New York: Harper Collins.

Davidson, R. 2012. *The Emotional Life of Your Brain*. New York: Avery.

De Ropp, Robert S. 1968. *The Master Game: Pathways to Higher Consciousness beyond the Drug Experience*. New York: Delacorte Press.

———. 1976. *Drugs and the Mind*. New rev. ed. New York: Delacorte Press.

Derrida, J. 1972. "Structure, Sign, and Play in the Discourse of Human Sciences." In R. Macksey and E. Canato (eds.), *The Structuralist Controversy*. Baltimore, MD: Johns Hopkins.

Eckhart, M. 1924. *Meister Eckhart*. Vol. 1. Trans. C. Evans. London: John M. Watkins.

Erikson, E. 1950. *Childhood and Society*. New York: Norton.

Feyerabend, Paul. 1993. *Against Method: Outline of an Anarchistic Theory of Knowledge*. 3rd ed. London: Verso.

Fink, Eugen. 2016. *Play as Symbol of the World and Other Writings*. Trans. Alexander Moore and Christopher Turner. Bloomington: Indiana University Press.

———. 1960. "Ontology of Play." *Philosophy Today* 4, no. 2: 95.

Fox, M. 1981. *Meditations with Meister Eckhart*. Rochester, VT: Bear and Company.

Frankl, Viktor. 1959. *Man's Search for Meaning*. Trans. Ilsa Lasch. Boston: Beacon.

Freud, Sigmund. 1958. *On Creativity and the Unconscious*. Trans. Joan Riviere. Intro. Benjamin Nelson. New York: Harper and Row Torchbooks.

———. 1961/1920. *Beyond the Pleasure Principle*. Trans. James Strachey. New York: Liveright.

Goffman, Erving. 1959. *The Presentation of Self in Everyday Life*. Garden City, NJ: Doubleday-Anchor.

———. 1967. *Interaction Ritual*. Garden City, NJ: Doubleday-Anchor.

Goldstein, Elisha. 2012. *The Now Effect: How a Mindful Moment Can Change the Rest of Your Life*. New York: Atria.

Goleman, Daniel, and Richard Davidson. 2017. *Altered Traits: Science Reveals How Meditation Changes Your Mind, Brain, and Body*. New York: Avery.

Grof, Stanislav. 1998. *The Cosmic Game*. Albany: State University of New York Press.

Grolnick, S., and L. Barkin, eds. 1988. *Between Reality and Fantasy.* Northvale, NJ: Aronson.
Groos, K. 1901. *The Play of Man.* Trans. E. Baldwin. New York: Appleton.
Guyer, Paul. 1997. *Kant and the Claims of Taste.* 2nd ed. Cambridge: Cambridge University Press.
Haley, Jay. 1963. *Strategies of Psychotherapy.* New York: Grune and Stratton.
Hans, James S. 1990. *The Fate of Desire.* Albany: State University of New York Press.
Harris, Sam. 2004. *The End of Faith: Religion, Terror, and the Future of Reason.* New York: Norton.
Hospers, John, ed. 1969. *Introductory Readings in Aesthetics.* New York: Collier-Macmillan.
Huzinga, J. 1955. *Homo Ludens.* Boston: Beacon.
Hyers, M. Conrad. 1974. *Zen and the Comic Spirit.* London: Rider & Co.
Johnstone, Brick, and Daniel Cohen. 2019. *Neuroscience, Selflessness, and Spiritual Experience: Explaining the Science of Transcendence.* London: Academic Press.
Kant, Immanuel. 1978. *The Critique of Judgement.* Trans. James Creed Meredith. Oxford: Oxford University Press.
Kariel, Henry. 1989. *The Desperate Politics of Post-Modernism.* Amherst: University of Massachusetts Press.
Knott, K. 1998. *Hinduism: A Very Short Introduction.* Oxford: Oxford University Press.
Koestler, A. 1976. *The Ghost in the Machine.* New York: Random House.
Korsmeyer, Caroline. 1998. *Aesthetics: The Big Questions.* Oxford: Blackwell.
Lehman, H., and P. Witty. 1927. *The Psychology of Play Activities.* New York: A. S. Barnes.
Leonard, Linda S. 1989. *Witness to the Fire: Creativity and the Veil of Addiction.* Boston: Shambhala.
MacIntyre, Alasdair C., and Kelvin Knight. 1998. *The MacIntyre Reader.* Notre Dame, IN: University of Notre Dame Press.
Mead, G. 1934. *Mind, Self, and Society.* Chicago: University of Chicago Press.
Millar, S. 1974. *The Psychology of Play.* New York: Jason Aronson.
Miller, D. 1969. *God and Games.* New York: World Publishing.
Misra, R. S. 1998. *The Integral Advaitism of Sri Aurobindo.* Motilal Banarsidass.
Montaigne, M. 1993. *The Essays: A Selection.* Trans. M. A. Screech. New York: Penguin.
Nietzsche, F. 1954. *The Portable Nietzsche.* Trans. Walter Kaufmann. New York: Penguin.
———. 1960. *The Joyful Wisdom.* Trans. T. Common. New York: Frederick Ungar.
Oriard, M. 1991. *Sporting with the Gods.* Cambridge: Cambridge University Press.
Perry, W. 1986. *A Treasury of Traditional Wisdom.* San Francisco: Harper and Row.
Piaget, J. 1951. *Play, Dreams and Imitation in Childhood.* Trans. C. Gattegno and F. Hodgson. New York: Norton.
Popper, K. 1998. *The World of Parmenides: Essays on the Presocratic Enlightenment.* Ed. Arne Peterson. New York: Routledge.

Rahner, H. 1967. *Man at Play*. Trans. B. Battershaw and E. Quinn. New York: Herder and Herder.

Rexroth, Kenneth. 1987. *World Outside the Window: Selected Essays of Kenneth Rexroth*. New York: New Directions.

Sax, W. S., ed. 1995. *The Gods at Play: Lila in South Asia*. Oxford: Oxford University Press.

Schiller, F. 1967. *On the Aesthetic Education of a Man in a Series of Letters*. Trans. E. M. Wilkinson and L. A. Willoughby. Oxford: Clarendon.

Schweig, G. M. 2005. *Dance of Divine Love: The Rasa Lila of Krishna*. Princeton, NJ: Princeton University Press.

Sloek, J. 1996. *Devotional Language*. Trans. H. Mossin. New York: Walter de Gruyter.

Smith, Jean, ed. 1999. *Radiant Mind: Essential Buddhist Teachings and Texts—A Tricycle Book*. New York: Riverhead Trade.

Spariosu, Mihai. 1989. *Dionysus Reborn: Play and the Aesthetic Dimension in Modern Philosophical and Scientific Discourse*. Ithaca, NY: Cornell University Press.

———. 1991. *God of Many Names: Play, Poetry, and Power in Hellenic Thought from Homer*. Durham, NC: Duke University Press.

———. 1997. *The Wreath of Wild Olive: Play, Liminality, and the Study of Literature*. Albany: State University of New York Press.

Sri Aurobindo. 1990. *The Life Divine*. Twin Lakes, WI: Lotus Press.

Stace, Walter T. 1960. *The Teachings of the Mystics*. New York: Mentor Books, 1960.

Stolnitz, Jerome. 1960. *Aesthetics and the Philosophy of Art Criticism*. Boston: Houghton-Mifflin.

Sutton-Smith, Brian. 1997. *The Ambiguity of Play*. Cambridge, MA: Harvard University Press.

Suurmond, J.-J. 1994. *Word and Spirit at Play*. Trans. J. Bowden. Grand Rapids, MI: Eerdmans.

Szasz, Thomas. 1967. *The Myth of Mental Illness*. New York: Dell.

Thurman, Robert. 2005. *Liberation upon Hearing in the Between: Living with the Tibetan Book of the Dead*. Boulder, CO: Sounds True Audio CD.

Tolle, Eckhart. 1997. *The Power of Now: A Guide to Spiritual Enlightenment*. Vancouver: Namaste.

Turner, Victor. 1967. *The Forest of Symbols*. Ithaca, NY: Cornell University Press.

———. 1987. "Betwixt and Between: The Liminal Period in Rites of Passage." In L. Mahdi, S. Foster, and M. Little (eds.), *Betwixt and Between: Patterns of Masculine and Feminine Initiation*. La Salle, IL: Open Court.

Vaillant, G. E. 2008. *Spiritual Evolution: A Scientific Defense of Faith*. New York: Harmony.

Vauchez, A. 2012. *Francis of Assisi: The Life and Afterlife of a Medieval Saint*. Trans. Michael Cusato. New Haven, CT: Yale University Press.

Walle, A. H. 1992. "William James' Legacy to Alcoholics Anonymous." *Journal of Addictive Diseases* 11, no. 3: 91–99.

Walsh, Roger. 1999. *Essential Spirituality: The Seven Central Practices to Awaken Heart and Mind.* New York: Wiley.

Wenner, Melinda. 2009. "The Serious Need for Play." *Scientific American*, February, 22–29.

Wilber, Ken. 1995. *Sex, Ecology, and Spirituality: The Spirit of Evolution.* Boston: Shambhala.

———. 1996. *A Brief History of Everything.* Boston: Shambhala.

———. 1997. *The Eye of the Spirit.* Boston: Shambhala.

Winnicott, Donald. 1971. *Playing and Reality.* New York: Basic Books.

Zander, R., and B. Zander. 2000. *The Art of Possibility.* Boston: Harvard Business School Press.

Index

AA. *See* Alcoholics Anonymous
acceptance, 122–23, 125, 128;
   Epictetus, 33; meditation, 71–72; *vs.*
   passivity, 126–27
addiction, 54–55, 66; frivolity, 55;
   meditation, mirror-image of, 71;
   model of all cravings, 76; opioids for
   pain, 141–43; willpower, 68–69
adulthood and play, 20, 71, 115
Albee, Edward, 50
alcohol. *See* addiction
Alcoholics Anonymous (AA), 49,
   66–69, 73, 76
altered state of consciousness:
   from meditation, 105, 138; from
   substances, 55, 104, 138
aporia, 6, 37
Aquinas, Thomas, 7, 13
Aristotle, 7, 13
Armstrong, Karen, 75, 92, 116, 117, 123
asceticism, 101; Besht, 86; Buddha,
   72, 101–2; Christianity, 12–13;
   Hinduism, 83
"as if" attitude, 38, 118–19; God's
   attitude, 38–39; pragmatism, 69;
   pluralism, 69
atheism, in response to postmodernism, 3
attachment: *vs.* emptiness, 109; facing
   death, 127. *See also* detachment
Augustine of Hippo, 12, 78, 129–30

aversion response, 142

Bateson, Gregory, 49
beauty, as aspect of compassion, 111
Berger, Peter, 121
Besht, 85–88
bodhisattva, 108, 111, 122
bright play, 75–98
Brown, Stuart, 24, 26–27, 77–78
Buber, Martin, 88–89
Buddha, 67, 72, 101–2
Buddhism, 67, 71–72, 92–93, 101–2,
   106–12; acceptance, 126–27;
   bodhisattva, 108, 111, 122; tantric
   Buddhism, 92–93, 136; terminology,
   108; Zen Buddhism, 102, 106–8

Campbell, Joseph, 116, 129
Camplin, Troy, 36–38
cancer, 125–30; acceptance approach,
   128; domination approach, 128
Catholicism, 1, 101. *See also*
   Christianity
certainty *vs.* doubt, 2, 14, 51, 97,
   118–19; Augustine *vs.* Plotinus, 78;
   benefits of, 97–98; false, 117–18; *vs.*
   play, 51; after postmodernism, 2–3;
   Socrates, 14; uncertainty as "as if,"
   37–38; uncertainty as liminal space,
   6–7, 22, 79. *See also* uncertainty

Chesterston, G. K., 37
childhood, 115; and aggression, 44–48; and certainty, 3; function of play, 14–24; lack of play and mental health, 26–27; and liminality, 5
Christianity, 12, 89–92, 117; Francis of Assisi, 90–91; Meister Eckhart, 91–92
Chrysostom, 12
Claparede, Edouard, 15–16
compassion: in AA, 69, 76, 95–96; *vs.* attachment, 112; bodhisattva, 109; in Buber, 88–89; in Buddhism, 92; as definition of spirituality, 76, 92; *vs.* dogma, 75; and emptiness, 107–8, 109–10; in Francis of Assisi, 90–91; Golden Rule, 92; in Hinduism, 80, 83–84; in meditation, 107–8; in *metta*, 107, 136–37; in mysticism, 95; in psychotherapy, 63–65; and service, 110. *See also* service
competition, 44–45; Lombardi, 50; Nietzsche, 49
connectedness, 109–10, 120–21; I-Thou, 88–89
cravings, 66–67, 71; as tar baby, 72
Creation: as aimless, 40; as fun, 76; as plan, 80, 92; as play, 39–40, 80–82, 91–92
cross-cultural issues, 2, 59; difference *vs.* domination, 60
cruelty, 47, 57. *See also* competition; dominance; patriarchy

dabbling, in response to postmodernism, 3, 4
Dalai Lama, 102
dark play, 43–56
Dass, Ram, 122
death, 127–29
detachment, 65, 70, 109, 127, 140; and compassion, 112; God as, 85; in meditation, 104, 106
Dewey, John, 67–69; power of habit, 68
Diogenes Laertius, 7

dominance, 45–46, 58; in male culture, 45–47, 60; in traditional cultures, 49
doubt: acceptance of, 119; denial of, 118. *See also* uncertainty
drugs. *See* addiction

Eagleton, Terry, 36
economic stress, 2
ego: goal of happiness, 73; not fighting, 73; as protector, 67; as tar baby, 67, 76
ego-transformation, 38, 56; definition, 75; as goal of spirituality, 75; similarity to play, 76–80
emptiness: and compassion, 107–8; as non-attachment, 109
Enlightenment (historical period), 4
enlightenment (satori), 75, 82–83, 101–3; goal of meditation, 107–11, 140
Epictetus, 32–33
Erikson, Erik, 20
ethics. *See* service
evolution, 39–40, 48, 95–96
existentialism, 34–35

failure: as humiliation, 44; as stepping-stone, 60
Fink, Eugen, 23–24
Flanking, 65–73; change in circumstances, 68; distraction, 65, 68; meditation as, 106; *vs.* willpower, 68–69
Forbes, Malcolm, 49
Francis of Assisi, 90–91
Frankl, Victor, 35
freedom: Frankl, 35; Hegel, 39; Nietzsche, 39–40. *See also* possibility
Freud, Sigmund, 16–17
frivolity, 52–53
fun: and dark play, 44–45, 52–55; Erikson, 20; as feature of play, 5, 76, 77–78; Francis of Assisi, 90; as a good, 91–92, 95–96; Huizinga, 18; as inferior, 12–13; as liminal,

6; and meditation, 103–5, 132, 134; Merry Pranksters, 52; and religion, 77–78, 80; socializing function, 28; Socrates, 14; and work, 9–10
functional psychology, 68
fundamentalism, 78–79, 85, 119, 120; and postmodernism, 3. *See also* "as if" attitude; certainty; imaginativeness; literalism

games/gaming: in child development, 19–20; hide-and-seek, 43–45, 81, 87–88, 95; *vs.* play, 44–45, 49–50, 70
given reality. *See* acceptance
God: as detached, 85; as force *vs.* person, 40, 94–95; as player, 38–39; as "playmate," 104, 138; as providing the playing field, 33, 76. *See also* Creation
Goenka, S. N., 66, 112
Golden Rule, 92
Goldstein, Elisha, 106
gopi, 81
growth mentality, 60

Harris, Sam, 110
Hasidism. *See* Besht
Hegel, Georg, 39–40
Heraclitus, 7, 34
hide-and-seek, 43–45, 88; *gopis,* 81, Messiah, 87–88; mysticism, 95
hierarchies, 11, 48, 60
Hinduism, 80–85
Holocaust, 35
hospitality, 59
Huizinga, Johan, 18

imaginativeness, 5, 35–37, 78–79; as basis of all religion, 116–17; Besht, 88; in child development, 16–17, 19–21; as feature of play, 5; Francis of Assisi, 90; meditation, 105; mysticism, 93–94; from uncertainty, 69, 119. *See also* "as if" attitude

impermanence, 7, 71–72, 107
in-betweenness. *See* liminality

James, William, 69
Judaism, 85–89

Kali (goddess), 82–84; lila of, 83
Kamalasila, 109
Kane, Pat, 36–37
Kishitigarbha, 111
Kushner, Jared, 53–54

lila, 80–82
liminality: as another reality, 21, 36; in childhood play, 21–23; as feature of play, 5–6, 7; in meditation, 105–6, 109, 127; as non-reactivity, 106; risks, 7, 55; in spirituality, 79–80; unbalanced in dark play, 55
literalism in religion, 96, 117–18, 119–20; *vs.* values, 118. *See also* "as if" attitude
Lombardi, Vince, 50

masculinity: and aggression, 46–48; and connection, 47; *vs.* patriarchy, 58
McGonigal, Kelly, 141–42
McCarthy, Joseph, 2, 48
Mead, George Herbert, 17–18
meditation, 102–8; addiction, mirror-image of, 71; as flanking, 70; how to meditate, 131–40; as non-dual play, 73; play/sports, similarity to, 70–71; research on, 141–43; types of, 135–38
Meister Eckhart, 91–92
mental health: lack of play, 24–25; living with uncertainty, 6–7
Merry Pranksters, 52–53
metta, 107, 110, 136–37
Misra, Ram Shanker, 81
Montaigne, Michel de, 79
mysticism, 93–95

narcissism, 53–54

Nichtern, Ethan, 127
Nietzsche, Friedrich, 28, 34, 40–41; and competition, 49
non-dominance, 61–65. *See also* flanking
non-dualism, 73
non-reactivity, 72, 126; during meditation, 106, 135

observation: in meditation, 71–72, 104; in open-monitoring meditation, 135; and pain, 128
obsession, 54–55; *vs.* freedom, 55
Onken, Orrin, 68–69

pain: mental aspect, 142; observation, 128; research on, 141–43; *vs.* suffering, 109, 122, 128, 139, 142, 143
participation: in Buddhism, 93; *vs.* compulsion, 67, 117; as feature of play, 5; in Francis of Assisi, 90; in Hinduism, 80; in meditation, 103; in spirituality, 77
patriarchy, 46–48
Piaget, Jean, 18
Plato, 6, 13
platypus, 40
play: features of, 5–7; hide-and-seek, 43–45, 88; and mental health, 24–25; in politics, 52–53; research on, 24–25, 27; as spirituality, 76–80, 116. *See also* rationality; theories of play; work
pleasure: *vs.* addiction/decadence, 45, 55, 139; in childhood, 16–17; as evil, 13. *See also* fun
possibility: in play, 31–41; in Hinduism, 80
postmodernism, 96–97; definition, 3–4; effect on faith, 2
power. *See* domination
psychotherapy, 24, 49, 138–39; acceptance and commitment therapy, 128; examples, 24–27, 61–65

Ramakrishna, 84
randomness, 39; in evolution, 39–40, 48
rationality: limits of, 68–69; *vs.* play, 13
reactivity, 72, 126; during meditation, 106, 135
religion: affected by postmodernism and stress, 2–3; as game, 50–51; providing rest, 51, 97
research: on meditation, 141–43; on play, 24–25, 27
responsibility of humans, 85
Robinson, Edward Arlington, 31–32
Rohr, Richard, 7, 37

Schiller, Friedrich, 31, 36
science: evolution, 39; intelligent design, 40; meditation, 141–43; neuroscience, 95–96, 143; time, 129–30
service: in AA, 69, 76; in Buddhism, 111; in Christianity, 75, 111; as definition of ego-transformation, 75; *vs.* ego, 75; in Islam, 75; in Judaism, 87; to others, 110–12. *See also* bodhisattva
sex, 92–93
Shaw, Miranda, 92–93
signal of transcendence, 121
skepticism, two sides of, 4, 121
smoking. *See* addiction
social Darwinism, 48
Socrates, 6, 13–14
Spariosu, Mihai, 36–38
spirituality, definition of, 38. *See also* ego-transformation
Spong, John Shelby, 119
sports: analogy to play, 33–34; like meditation, 70, 103, 135; and masculinity, 47; as relational, 89; as source of transcendence, 108
Sri Aurobindo, 81
Stoics, 32–33
St. Francis. *See* Francis of Assisi
St. Paul, 12
suffering: alleviating, 112, 136–37; Besht, 86; bodhisattva, 111–12;

Buddha, 101–2; and cravings, 66–67; limits of rationality, 26; limits of willpower, 67; as religious problem, 3; source of, 71, 109. *See also* pain

Sutton-Smith, Brian, 50

tantric Buddhism, 92–93, 136

tar baby, as symbol of entanglement, 56, 67, 72, 126

Teismann, Mark: cancer, 125–30; compassion, understanding of, 139–40; friend Sam (addiction), 66–67; meditation, 66, 71–72, 138–40; religious beliefs, 101; seminary, 28; therapy work, 24–26, 61–65. *See also* Teismann, Mark, childhood memories

Teismann, Mark, childhood memories: ants (flanking, masculinity), 57–61, 65; Catholic school (spiritual play), 1; hide-and-seek (competition), 43–45; lawn-mowing (play *vs.* work), 9–10

theology, as play, 38. *See also* "as if" attitude

theories of play: as absorbing external reality, 18–19, 21–22; balancing, 13–14; compensatory, 16, 47; developmental, 16, 18, 20; as drive, 36, 37; epistemological, 36; evil, 12–13; evolutionary, 15; fun, 18, 20; relaxation, 15; rung view, 14–23; transitional, 22; venting, 16

Thurman, Robert, 107

Tollner, Johann, 12–13

toxic masculinity, 45–46

Trinity, 91–92

Trump, Donald, 54

Turner, Victor, 5

twelve-step programs, 67–69; and service, 76. *See also* Alcoholics Anonymous

uncertainty: and imagination, 69, 119; as manipulation, 54; in meditation, 134–35; as play, 37, 76; and postmodernism, 2–3; in science, 118. *See also* certainty

Vaillant, George, 95–96

Vipassana meditation, 66, 71–72, 106, 112

Wenner, Melinda, 26–27

"what if" attitude, 35–41. *See also* "as if" attitude

Whitman, Charles, 26, 77

wild play, 52–55

willpower, limits of, 66, 68–69, 72

Wilson, Bill, 69

Winnicott, Donald, 21–23

winning. *See* competition

work, in contrast with play, 9–14, 11–12, 13–14

Xenophon, 7

yoga, 84–85. *See also* tantric Buddhism

Zen Buddhism, 102, 106–8

About the Authors

Mark W. Teismann was a college basketball star, then medical student, who later studied to become a Catholic priest, ultimately leaving that trajectory to become an innovator, educator, and practicing psychotherapist. He taught at Northern Illinois University, where he was a professor, founder of the training program in family and marital therapy, and director of the Family Center. For more than four decades he maintained a large and intense private therapy practice. His research and writing focused on the philosophy, theology, and psychology of play. He meditated daily, more or less in the Buddhist Vipassana tradition of insight meditation. In 2015 he moved through his final threshold after a diagnosis of gastroesophageal cancer, inspiring and amazing many folks on his "team." After his death, his wife Ruth Jackson and friend Howard Waitzkin gathered together his writings and notes that

Mark intended for use in a book on play in spirituality and made the present volume possible.

Lynn Weber has worked for many years as a writer and editor. She has been a book reviewer for the esteemed journal *Booklist* and now specializes in helping authors bring their book ideas to fruition through consultation, substantive editing, and cowriting. She has an upcoming memoir to be published in 2020.

www.ingramcontent.com/pod-product-compliance
Lightning Source LLC
Chambersburg PA
CBHW050908300426
44111CB00010B/1438